ANGEL IN ARMOR

A Post-Freudian Perspective on the Nature of Man

D1488291

ANGEL IN ARMOR

A Post-Freudian Perspective on the Nature of Man

ERNEST BECKER

The Free Press
A Division of Macmillan Publishing Co., Inc.
New York

Collier Macmillan Publishers
London

The Free Press
A Division of Macmillan Publishing Co., Inc.
866 Third Avenue, New York, N.Y. 10022

Collier-Macmillan Canada Ltd.

Library of Congress Catalog Card Number: 69–12803
Free Press Paperback Edition, 1975

Printed by arrangement with George Braziller, Inc.

Printed in the United States of America

printing number
1   2   3   4   5   6   7   8   9   10

The author wishes to thank the publishers of Franz Kafka's "The Judgment: a Story for F." for permission to quote from their editions. The short story appears in Franz Kafka, *The Penal Colony,* copyright © 1948, by Schocken Books, Inc; in England in Franz Kafka, *In the Penal Settlement: Tales and Short Prose Works,* London: Martin Secker and Warburg, 1949.

To the memory of

Emmanuel Mounier

rare thinker of our time who kept alive the vision

that the study of man is also a struggle *for* man

Preface

The essays in this book fit well into an approach that is now called "existential psychology" or "third-force" psychology. But the new words, and the dispute in psychology that they represent, should not blind us to the long tradition behind them. They are a modern statement of the characterology that developed in the earlier part of this century, and that has been quietly maturing behind the scene. This earlier tradition began with people like Rousseau and Fourier, and stretched through the "Personalism" of Borden Bowne, Josiah Royce, Dilthey, Eduard Spranger, on up to Emmanuel Mounier. These were large men who thought largely about their world, about man's character and his fate. They represented a tradition of knowledge whose aim was to educate, elevate, and free man, and not to placate, constrict, and package him. This tradition was so long and unjustly eclipsed by many other players who occupied the glare of the front of the modern stage: medical psychiatry, which can only think in terms of biology, and operates naïvely under a metaphysics of pan-reductionism; medical psychiatry's willing ally—a dogmatic Freudianism with its pansexual mystique and its own pan-reductionism. Also allied with them full in the floodlights is the never-ending stream of instant books by zoologists, biologists, and journalists, who popularize a "nothing-but" image of man for the amusement and cynical peace of mind of the mass audience: man is "nothing-but" an ape in evening clothes, or a baboon who has made sex sophisticated and fighting more deadly; or finally, a gibbon in whom nature has indelibly planted a sense of territory, and whose destiny it has been to translate it into the eternal trinity: home, mother, and flag.

Crowded on the stage with these virtuoso players, but behind them like a huge, faceless symphony orchestra, has been the horde of busy specialists and narrow technicians in the various disciplines that have studied man. Each asked nothing better than to be given a tiny piece of the score, a small area where one could minutely examine a facet of the human image—and the tinier the better. Little did it matter that there was no leader for this cacophony—no vision of man by which to order all the fragmented, separate work, no way to evaluate it. There was plenty of money to carry on the most mindless research, plenty of students to foist it upon, and there seemed to be an eternity in which to work.

But now we are finding that the money is going increasingly to other more deadly kinds of national amusement; that the students who were content to quietly lament and privately question, are loudly complaining and publicly accusing. In the present crisis, in short, time is running out. Which means that we must get back to basic perspectives and truly cumulative knowledge. If these essays contribute something toward this aim, they will be more than justified.

The first essay, on the perversions, was written half a dozen years ago, and has since been mined for other writings, especially some of the views I recently published in *The Structure of Evil*. Perhaps I should have followed the urgings of modesty and caution in the face of the deluge of publications in our time, and let this earlier essay continue its peaceful repose in a desk drawer. But I decided to publish it, even though parts of it have been duplicated and extended in subsequent writings, because it provides a background for the other essays in this volume, still stands on its own as a composite theoretical statement, and contains some views not previously published.

The next three essays were originally given in the form of lectures to students over the past few years, and it was at the urging of some that I have committed them to writing. As lectures in courses on human behavior they were designed to provide an emotional closure on an intellectual approach, to get as close as we can to a rounded educational experience. As such they were very successful, to judge by student response and by my own pleasure in giving them. I am hopeful that they will be the same in their present written form.

The final essay represents my most recent and considered thinking on the problem of human nature, and on the politics of our failure to present an agreed image of man to the anguished and cheated youth of our time. Like all my other work, these essays are really addressed only to them.

—E.B.

San Francisco, Summer, 1968

Contents

I | EVERYMAN AS PERVERT

An Essay on the Pathology of Normalcy

Manias are diminutive passions,
the result of man's need to create stimulants
for himself.

CHARLES FOURIER *(1849, p. 233)*

The sense of reality is the sense of effectiveness . . .

ALFRED NORTH WHITEHEAD *(1958, p. 167)*

TODAY WHEN we talk about the sexual perversions, in the human sciences, we risk eliciting a yawn—the matter seems so cut and dried. With monotonous regularity psychiatrists and psychoanalysts have classified these behaviors to accord with textbook explanations, and with the theory of instincts and the Oedipus complex. And so we have the so-called "classic" explanations, "classic" implying that the matter is settled once and for all, and can hardly be improved upon. In psychoanalytic theory, for example, the phenomenon of fetishism is explained on the basis of castration anxiety, and goes something like this:

The fetish object, say, a shoe, is considered to be a visual substitute for the penis. The logic that is supposed to go on in the fetishist's unconscious is simple: "I see the shoe (penis), therefore this woman is not castrated—that is to say, I have visual proof that castration as a punishment for copulation does not exist. Hence, the fetish object is my 'permission to copulate' without fear of castration."

Remarkable things can surely be done with Freud's theory of the Oedipus complex, as this formulation suggests. Scientists of man of the future will marvel at the perversity of his own ingenuity, even while they give him credit for his true greatness. The judgment on him may well be similar to that on Charles Fourier: a powerful genius, sound in his basic ideas and intuitions, unbelievably liberating to the human spirit, and yet incredibly inverted upon the formulations of his own closed theory. The problem of Freud, as of all science, is to keep what is basic, while breaking out of the confines of a too narrow and constricting general theory. All this has been well said before, but it applies especially to the theory of the perversions, which I want to discuss.

To mention Fourier and Freud in the same breath helps us set the keynote for our discussion, by letting the proper amount of light on the problem. The fact is that in order to go beyond Freud, we have to go back before him to the nineteenth century, the time when human behavior problems were cogitated with a broadness that has been lacking since the beginning of this century, and which we are only now winning back. The reign of medical psychiatry and the enthronement of a dogmatic psychoanalysis have practically stifled our understanding of what is truly fundamental about human behavior. Today we know that in order to get back to the empirical reality, we have to peel off some of the scales of psychiatry and psychoanalysis, and reach out to fields like philosophy and social psychology. We have again to pay tribute to men like Fourier, and Vladimir Soloviev, and J. M. Baldwin, who understood aspects of the perversions with a penetration that medical men may well envy, and that modern students must respect. There was a time when the philosopher Soloviev dared to disagree with the whole corpus of "scientific" work on the sexual perversions. Soloviev said that if we make love to a woman without relating to her spirit, we are fetishists, even if in the physical act we use the proper body orifice. I hope that my brief essay will help the student understand what he meant, as well as give him the same courage in the face of "expert" and incrusted theory.

In the last two decades there has been a great stirring to re-evaluate the theory of the perversions, and to try to explain what they really mean, without the prejudices of medicine or of dogmatic psychoanalysis. This stirring has come principally from what is known as existential psychiatry and phenomenological philosophy. What they have tried to do, simply, is to look at what the world means to the experiencing subject, in the total context of his action. Like Fourier in the nineteenth century, they have enunciated a principle of Absolute Doubt of all pre-existing formulations; they are setting out to see what raw experience means, without superimposing any ready-made theory from the outside. Some of the important names in this new tradition, which we will touch on in the following pages, are Médard Boss, Sartre, and Simone de Beauvoir—all of whom we might classify as existential phenomenologists. All in all, they have provided us with a fairly thoroughgoing critique of the psychoanalytic theory of perversions, as well as their own formulations. Even more popular philosophers like Colin Wilson have contributed criticism and insights to this tradition.

But there has also been some stirring from within traditional psychiatry; I refer to Simon Nagler's important recent paper (1957), in which he reviewed the psychoanalytic literature and observed that it was not until 1939 that the analytic writings suggested that personality development and fetishism were related. He concluded, like the existential phenomenologists, that fetishism is not merely a narrow aspect of psychosexual development, but part of a whole life style, "a special kind of consciousness" (p. 737).

Taking my cue from these sources of reappraisal, I want to throw some of my own perspectives on the principal problems underlying human striving, feeling free to lean heavily on some common philosophical ideas. As I hope to show, not only do they confirm what the existentialists and phenomenologists are finding, but they give us a fairly complete framework for a general theory of the perversions. There is nothing today to prevent an amalgamation of the views of the above-cited people. That there could be a convergence of people from such diverse areas of work and thought, from the most expert to the most generalist-popular, is itself a strong argument for moving on to a new general theory.

The Problem of Meaning

The first thing we must do to orient ourselves to the new approaches, is to habituate ourselves to thinking in terms of the *individual subject,* the acting organism who is trying to negotiate his world, come to terms with it, with the plenitude of objects in it. The organism is immersed in nature, and builds its life by transacting with a domain of organic and inorganic things. The problem of the "meaning of life," for the organism, reduces itself to the terms on which the organism acts in the world. What makes life "meaningful" to the acting organism? Simply, that which secures and guarantees the forward momentum of its action. Meaning, in other words, must be understood behaviorally. Only in this way can we make sense of the sometimes peculiar efforts and contortions by means of which man strives for meaning. An object has meaning for me, the acting organism, if I can predict the consequences of my behavior toward it—if I can predict its effect on me, or my effect on it. The subject creates a cause-and-effect world by assessing his powers in relation to the many different objects in his field. He builds up a framework of meaning, which is nothing more than a framework of confident expectation in relation to action and objects. Since, as Bergson stressed, action is life, meaning for any organism is simply the possibility of action; in simple terms, action = life = meaning.

"We're getting on!" said the lead character in Samuel Beckett's *Endgame,* gleefully rubbing his hands as he repeated it. To "get on" is to earn organismic meaning in the most direct sense. Besides, it is the only way we know how. For an energy-converting organism, to live is to move forward. This is our lifelong imperative; to violate it is to die. Beckett is painfully sensitive to this very truth: that man is driven by an imperative that he can neither understand nor rebel against; and he dresses this imperative in the flimsiest and most transparent garb: human word-noise.

To negotiate dependable action, then, is to imbibe in meaning; to build up a world of known and expected consequences is to create meaning. The network of sequences within which we plot our lives is the only fabric of meaning we can know. But, man "gets on" not only actively, in relation to external objects in his external behavioral field, but also passively, in relation to symbols, words, and images—ideational objects in his internal mental field. Language forms a logically coherent system which, if one follows the rules of syntax, creates its own dependable satisfactions. Nouns are referred to adjectives, we can skip from subjects to objects, predicates, connectives— a lively ideational world which keeps us moving meaningfully over an entire field of intricate stimulation. Furthermore, words stand for objects, and we can move gracefully from the internal world of meaning to the external one, in confidence that the expected connection will be made: "This is beach sand—it should be . . . warm."

None of this is, of course, new. It is a barest summary of William James's, James Mark Baldwin's, George Mead's, and John Dewey's views on the behavioral nature of meaning, which are now common currency in our thinking. But unless we continually think in terms of the organism's need to constitute meaning in order to act (live), we miss an essential problem of behavior: our relationships with objects.

The Problem of Objects

What makes an object meaningful? Simply, our ability to behave toward it. It has meaning if it rallies us to act. Thus, when we say that we "lack meaning" we are actually saying that we *lack dependable behavior patterns.* Our intricate framework of expected cause-and-effect sequences may be sparse, or it may be shattered and unsound. But whatever the trouble, this trouble translates itself directly into an inhibition of our powers to act. The meaning-framework in which we imbibe is composed of external objects and internal symbol objects. It is an ideational world inextricably woven into our neural networks. Nerve impulses, images, muscular tensions, real objects —it is these that form a tidy, self-consistent framework that composes our meaning world. But the important thing to note here is that if we lack the *dependable responses* to the objects, this is just another way of saying that we lack *the objects,* or that we lack *the meaning-framework.* The circle is self-reinforcing: the more objects we have, the more behavior we have, the more meaning we have (the more "life" we have). Meaning, behavior, and objects form the inseparable constitution of our world.

This leads us directly into the problem of mature object relations. What do we actually mean when we talk of "part objects" or "whole objects?" When we say that a patient relates to people only as "part objects," we mean precisely that he is able *to call up only a limited range of behaviors* with reference to them. This view is in direct agreement with psychoanalytic theory. Thus, to relate to a woman as though she were only a vessel in which to prove one's virility indicates that this is the only self-satisfying behavior that one really knows toward an object defined as a "woman." Each object has certain avenues of approach which are proper to it. These approaches—or proper behaviors—are what we learn in society. The more limited our experience with these avenues of approach, *the less* the object *exists* for us. We constitute a fuller object only to the extent that we *develop a broader spectrum of behavior* toward it. Instead of reducing the object to the narrowest possible aspect with which we can cope—say, sexuality in reference to a woman—we try to broaden our behavioral possibilities toward it. One's whole life, in fact, is just such an education, an education in broadening the range of one's behaviors toward objects.

An individual, then, with fewer dependable behavior patterns has less meaning in his world: fewer, poorer, shallower, more fragmentary objects.

The Problem of Separation

Now we can see more fully that a principal problem for the acting organism is that of constituting a rich, meaningful world to which he can be committed. For man, as compared to other organisms, the problem is even heightened. Of all mammals man is born and nurtured in closest, longest contact with a responsive object world. The human infant develops an amazingly acute sensorium, in contact with objects of the most minute differentia. Thus, the need for a continuingly rich, dependable, and varied object world seems logically to be at its greatest in the most psychologically sensitive of the mammals.

Man's efforts to span the distance between himself and objects is almost continual. This central problem of all of life is probably aggravated in man due to the lack of built-in instinctual pathways that guarantee contact with objects: the cat "knows" exactly how to react to its prey. The object is largely preconstituted *for* the cat, with a minimum of effortful learning or anxiety on its part. If man cannot rely on instincts to make his world rich and meaningful, he has to fall back on his senses; and as a descendant of the tree-living primates nature has endowed him with the queen of senses, acute vision. Perception is the sense that draws man into the world with great ease and compellingness; we can see that from earliest childhood the burden of wonder and discovery is on this sense. Every object, perceived, is a bridge by means of which isolation is overcome; every perception is a commitment to the world.

But we must be very cautious not to claim too much for the sense of sight. There is a critical paradox involved in it: it has to do almost everything to make the world meaningful and rich with objects; yet, by itself, it can do almost nothing. I mean that although perception is man's best sense, he lacks, as we said, the instinctive behavior patterns that would be automatically called into play by perception. The rub of the paradox is that *perception does not constitute the object*. The burden of constituting a true object as a bridge to the world must fall on the development of behavior patterns. In a word, there is nothing in man's naturally given world that relieves him of the need for constant struggle to ward off isolation, shallowness, poverty of meaning.

The Nature of Self-Esteem

The next important idea that we must arm ourselves with, in order to understand a perversion like fetishism, is the fundamental place that self-esteem has in human action. We must understand how important it is for the individual to feel himself a locus of value, to have a warm sense of his own worth. We know that he earns this from childhood on as he wins approval from his parents for his acts. But the thing we really have to understand about self-esteem is that it cannot be achieved in a passive way only. The organism is basically an active creature, and can best feel warm about itself as it senses the pleasures of exercising its executive powers. We know that our highest satisfactions can only derive from solid achievement, from testing ourselves against the world and proving our powers to it. This has been known for a very long time, but in today's world almost everything works to make people passive, and we need to be reminded of it most strongly. William Goldfarb has aptly rephrased Descartes's philosophical dictum for our time, to read: "I am doing, therefore I am" (1961, p. 26). It is the only way that makes sense to an active organism. Or as Paul Goodman also put it: "I have done that, therefore I am" (1962, p. 268).

The point we have to remember, then, is that self-esteem is inseparable from one's acts and one's power to act. If we are limited in executive behavior toward the object world, we are *ipso facto* low in self-esteem. We then have to contrive it somehow: and the record of that contriving is what we mean, largely, by perversions like fetishism.

Fetishism as Low Self-Esteem

Having struggled through these abstract and somewhat arid preparatory concepts, we are now ready to tackle the phenomenon of fetishism in some manner approximating its real nature. Nagler, in the important paper we cited earlier, makes a clean break with previous psychoanalytic explanations of fetishism as being a reflex of fear of castration or escape from the woman. From his own case work and from a nondogmatic weighing of the literature, Nagler is able to conclude that the fetishist is "an insecure, passive, dependent, and inadequate male, whose auto-erotic and diminished sexual activity is simply a reflection of general inactivity" (1957, p. 737). And if we often see fetishism merging with homosexuality and transvestitism, we know that this triad has one basic feature: "the fear of the male social role in its entirety in the face of an overwhelming sense of inadequacy and a low self-esteem."

How could it be otherwise? "General inactivity," "low self-esteem," and "sense of inadequacy" indicate that the fetishist is a person who has sentenced himself to live *in a certain kind of object world*. It will be shallow in terms of the complexity and richness of its objects; it will represent a narrow commitment instead of a broad and flexible one; yet, it will be *a segment* of the world which has to bear a full load of life meaning. In other words, the fetishist will be a behaviorally poor person, who has the resourceful task of creating a rich world. As we said, the record of that resourceful contriving is the fetish behavior itself.

"Normal" Fetishism

If fetishism, by definition, connotes the merger of poverty and ingenuity, we also know that none of us is exempt from the "disease." We are all relatively poor and ingenious. This is what permits us to handle, with full devotion and finely tuned capability, a very definite area of the object world. Without routine compulsiveness, we would all literally fade away; we would be able to marshal no ego at all. The more our powers are limited, and the more some special commitment is wanted, the more we become alert to fetishistic cues to action. They give us a quick definition, an easy commitment, a rapid summing-up of *just what powers and how much care* we need to bring to bear in a particular situation. Thus we are all more or less prone to fetishistic definitions in our sex life when we show a preference for a particular portion of our partner's body. There is nothing per se about a large breast that has any more inherent sexual stimulation to the partner than a small one. Obviously it is all in the eye of the beholder. But our culture teaches us to become committed in *some* way to the body of the opposite sex, and we are eager for cues which give us a passport to permissive excitation. When we learn such a cue, we invest it with rich significance. Each culture heightens the meaning of certain qualities of objects so that its members can easily bring into play the approved responsive behavior: lace underwear and steatopygia for sex objects, tailfins and chrome for cars. The easy mark of "beauty" that serves as a perceptual counter is a promise that socially approved satisfaction will be forthcoming. The identifying body part signals, in encapsulated form, an entire range of meanings—of cause-and-effect sequences to be expected. It is as though the individual says: "By focusing my attention on this, I can safely proceed to derive sexual satisfaction and fulfill the proper sex role."

One can easily see that in a very real sense, almost all of man's cultural life takes place on a fetishistic level. Philosophers have taught us that we can never know objects in all their potential fullness. As Diderot, Comte, Whitehead, and others understood, our nervous system itself is *already* a limitation, a sentence to a distorted and partial object world. We can respond to an object largely only in terms of what we *can do* to it, and in this we are limited by the inheritance of millions of years of adaptive evolution. By the very nature of our immersion in a limitless universe, while possessing only limited capacities, we are condemned to a "normal" fetishism. Our world has already been delivered to us abstracted. The mission of both science and art, as the highest human strivings, is to create new objects and to reveal facets of old objects that we did not know existed. The lower animals, after all, are fetishists par excellence: they are securely built into a limited range of responsiveness to the merest fragments of objects—an odor, a colored stripe, a hiss.

It is given to man alone to break out, somewhat, of the fetishistic world to which nature has condemned sense creatures.

The Fetish Object

The inanimate fetish object, then, is merely a further symbolic reduction of the fetishistic body part. For the extreme fetishist, it seems that even the organic body part itself, say, a breast, calls out a range of behavior that is too demanding or too threatening. It has been often noted that masturbation is nearly the sole sexual activity of the true fetishist, and this is what we would expect. When one relates to the object as a part object, whether it is an outsized breast or an inanimate object like a shoe, one is *essentially* masturbating. To the extent that one does not need "permission" to be sexual, or does not need a special body contour or identifiable object to trigger this behavior—to that extent one can relate to (more of) the totality of the other person, the sex partner. But, theoretically at any rate, *some* "masturbation" is implicit in using the body of the opposite sex for *some* clues—that is, *in having to identify the partner as a sex object at all.* That is to say, the very identification of the partner as a sex object invites a degree of inversion that we could consider masturbatory. Logically, this is unavoidable: if we were to relate to the object as a total object, *it would cease to be a sexual object at all.* Thus, in "normal" sexual behavior, we try to gain some approximation of a total relationship to the object, even while using an avenue of approach that inevitably reduces it initially to a part-object status.

The fetishist, then, as someone who is severely limited in his behavior, is not—as we stressed above—deprived of resource-fulness. On the contrary, being limited in behavior, he is tasked to create *an extra charge of life-enhancing meaning in a more limited area* than that necessary for the rest of us. That is to say, he must fix on some perceptual detail, and derive the *full justification for drawing himself to the object* from this very narrow focalization. It is this very resourcefulness that appears to the outsider as "abnormal." Let us try to imagine some of what is going on in the extreme fetishist's world. When he says "Your boots are driving me crazy!"[1] he is simply extending or varying the common remark: "Your breasts are driving me crazy!" The fetishist is being drawn perceptually (behaviorally) into the object world by this focal detail. Hence, the tantalizing, frustrating nature of the fetish object to the fetishist's craving. It is a *supercharged* locus of meaning, self-designated as of supreme importance for potential satisfaction. Obviously, the fetish object itself cannot conceivably fulfill the promise of satisfaction with which it has been burdened: hence, the fetish-ist is caught in a maddening bind. Of course the object is driving him crazy. He is forced to overinvest in the promise of the largely symbolic fetish object due to his own behavioral poverty; while, at the same time, this symbolic overinvestment cannot be actively repaid by transacting with the simple part object itself. A breast or a shoe simply cannot, by their nature, reward the promise the fetishist has read into them.[2] (How many youths have not been astonished and let down by their first full view of the long-coveted female breast: it seems so oddly without character, for an object that had been invested with so much promise. Compared to the woman's face, this blank expanse of flesh is almost insultingly poor.)

After all, the fetishist is not doing anything more than the street corner ogler of girls who whistles low and agitatedly shouts "Look at that!" By means of unique, exciting, and pleasure-promising objects we draw ourselves into the world, and it becomes alive. Our potential separation is overcome, we are recommitted to the life process, substantiated in the world by means of electric contact with another *real* object. We use the object, as we noted above, to draw ourselves directly into the world. Without objects to commit our attention and striving we do not exist. Experiments on sensory deprivation are interesting mainly in that they prove our plight, our utter dependence on the object world for the coming into being of our directive powers.

And so the fatal passivity of the fetishist. When we elaborate on a part object in order to draw ourselves into the world we are actually affirming our behavioral poverty. The fetishist is condemned to passivity, and reinforces his sentence. Since there is little that one *can do* to a part object because it represents the willful reduction of a situation that invites a fuller range of action, the fetishist is *necessarily passive.* The focal relationship to the part object, that is, blots out other whole areas of possible relationship, and one can muster only a part action. The masturbatory act is all that remains reasonably to be done in the face of a shoe or a corset.

The question that arises in all part-object relationships is this: How far can one narrow down his grip on the world, and *still be in it* in "human" fashion? The fetishist is said to be near to psychosis precisely because his wedge into the object world is so narrow. In extreme schizophrenia we see such a ludicrous narrowing down of the schizophrenic's hold on the world: he seems to be making last-ditch efforts to relate to whatever objects his powers can muster a response to—bits of debris to stuff into body crevices—ultimately his own excrement, anything tangible with which to come into safe manipulatory contact. This represents a degradation of his executive powers to the near-zero level, rather than any peculiarly "mental" aberration (see Becker, 1964).

Masochism and Sadism

These remarks about fetishism help us to understand a whole host of related behaviors, which reflect the same kind of problem. Once we get behind the impressive technical words like "phobia," "counterphobia," "obsession," "compulsion," "concretization" (in schizophrenia), we see that they all reflect the basic human situation: the attempt by a hypersensitive Homo sapiens, with only meager powers, to call up some kind of dependable, meaningful behavior, in a threatening world. How naturally the child becomes "phobic" by fixing the overwhelmingness of his world on the neighbor's dog. He takes all the threat and awe to which his weak and struggling ego is subject, and contains it by giving it a fixed locus. This enables him to recall it at will, think about it, fantasy it, and yet control it, and avoid it. "Danger is *there,* not here." (See Wolpe and Rachman's important paper, 1960.)

How naturally, too, the child is "masochistic": pinch him and poke him as he lies supinely, and he will—with cautious delight—ask for "more." It is only too obvious what his "masochism" is: a way of maintaining himself as a locus of attention, as an object to be related to, when he has no known and tested ways to establish and support a relationship. If he has to be pinched in turn by three persons in order to partake of their world, this is better than not being in it at all, since he has not yet learned to play bridge. His body is a trump card.

Is the child a "sadist" in his torture of cats and toads, in his dismemberment of insects? But what a feeling of centered power it gives, of control, of ability to make things move and squirm: he literally makes the world come alive with powerful sounds and frantic movements; he literally controls life, unleashes natural powers on the world, and establishes himself as someone to be reckoned with. And this with only a small ego, a little strength, a feeble defiance of the way things are: he can arrange nature on the basis of his own pristine and unknown powers.

Is the child "compulsive" in his arrangement of his toys, in replacing the soap and towel in the bathroom, closing down the toilet seat? But what a simple formula for making the world safe again, for feeling "good" about himself in the face of all the complex and threatening "do's" and "don't's" that refer to his own well-being. One proceeds the "correct" way in little things, and the big things are appeased and ordered. The child is a natural ritualist, a Confucian.

In these few remarks I am not pretending to reduce the

complex world of adult motivations to a childhood level; but only to show that what we see so plainly on the level of childhood, is the same basic thing that we see disguised in the adult. The adult phobias and obsessions are more disguised because they are interwoven with a more varied and responsible daily life; when they are severe, they are more crippling precisely because they interfere with other responsibilities, and there is usually no parent for the adult to turn to for a comforting pat on the head and assurance. When the adult is a masochist, the behavior and the reasons for it are the same as the child; but then it is the more ludicrous and pathetic, there is no way to "forgive" him for it by laughing it off. He should "know better," and if he wants to pay a prostitute fifty dollars for pinching his ears, then he must be "queer." If he is a sadist, it is usually no longer with toads and flies, but with other persons, and this is not something that can be shrugged off if these other persons complain to the police: toads may croak, but they don't talk.

After all, for the adult or the child, the object is a fearsome thing if one's powers to relate to it are limited. And where the world is fearsome, it has a seniority over the self, and one is devalued no matter how old he is. The adult masochist, like the child, cannot imagine that he has rights or powers to treat the world on his own. The thing to do, then, is to be ingratiating and complying, no matter what the other person asks. Although he may hurt you, he at least condescends to relate to you; and since you have no terms to pose for the relationship, you accept his. In proportion as one is helpless to initiate action in the face of the object, we might say that all objects are tigers. One has only to recall his first childhood experience in a graveyard, where everything one brushed against or glimpsed in the shadows was immeasurably greater than one's own powers. The more that is strange and threatening about the object to one who is not possessed of firm executive powers, the more insignificant one must feel.

We can understand some of the problems of homosexuality, too, on the basis of these remarks. As Frederick H. Allen has observed, in two excellent papers (1937; 1940), the homosexual is often a person who cannot stand being different from others. Thus, he denies his difference by merging with others who are like himself. One sees a similar phenomenon in all ego-weak individuals, whether young adolescents or schizophrenics, when they insist that they must communicate totally and understand totally their interlocutor. The ego-weak individual not only has to see himself in another, but he has to know all that the other is thinking. "Be me and I'll be you— and only then can we understand each other and feel free to transact with each other." These people cannot stand the difference that cuts them off from the object, that keeps it aloof and unplumbed. If there is anything private, anything unalike in their own natures or in the object, they feel threatened by the separation. Ego-weak children with contagious diseases often try to infect those around them: the strain of being separate, marked off, special, is too much for them.

So, in sum, when we talk about a variety of childishnesses, of "perversions," we are really talking about the same general kind of deficit; and it is a deficit, as we said earlier, in *be-havior:* in the range, broadness and flexibility of one's active powers. When these are at a minimum, even one's uniqueness can be a threat to oneself, because one cannot support the claim that difference thrusts upon him. We renounce personal claims precisely when we lack the initiatory powers necessary to sustain them. We are in the world on *its* terms, not on our own. And so we see various types of "empty" individuals, empty of power, of pretensions, of personal motives: homosexual ghosts who seem to say "I am like my partner—he like me"; trans-vestite ghosts, who seem to say: "I am like my clothes—my clothes *are* me"; and fetishist ghosts, who can argue: "I do not have to relate to this whole, awesome, and threatening person. I can render him manageable by taking this one narrow path of entry, which allows me to deal with him on some terms and get some satisfaction out of it for myself."

More Complex Aspects of Sadism and Masochism

By keeping our discussion on this general and simple level, I think we have been able to sum up a good deal of what lies behind the problem of human perversion. But in order to get a more complete understanding of phenomena like sadism and masochism as they exist in the adult, we have to introduce more theoretical complexity into the problem. Specifically, there are two major ways in which adult sadism and masochism differ from simple childish behavior. We might call them the "value aspect" of sado-masochism, and the "ontological aspect." The best recent discussions of these dimensions of the problem that

I know are by Sartre (1956), De Beauvoir (1953), and Boss (1949). I don't want to try to repeat or sum up the excellent things they have written; what I do want to do is to try to weave their views into an economical and coherent framework for a complete approach to the problem of sado-masochism.

The Value Aspect

The value aspect of sadism is summed up in the difference between the child and the adult: the adult lives in a cultural, abstract moral world; the child still lives in a world of concrete physical things. If the child rearranges the world he has been given, his rearrangement is still confined largely to the animals and insects he manipulates. When the adult attacks his world to affirm his own powers, it is the cultural, moral world that he defies. No one has understood this better than De Beauvoir, in her penetrating essay on Sade. What Sade hated were the man-made conventions that were imposed on the natural world. De Beauvoir says:

> The world to which he tried to adapt himself was . . . a world governed by those universal laws which he regarded as abstract, false, and unjust . . . Sade takes us to Tahiti, Patagonia, and the antipodes, to show us that the diversity of enacted laws definitively negates their value . . . they seem to him arbitrary. And it should be noted that for him the words "conventional" and "imaginary" are synonymous. Nature retains her sacred character for Sade; indivisible and unique, she is an absolute, outside of which there is no reality (1953, p. 61).

By desecrating what men have fashioned, Sade wants to affirm a more vital and basic reality. To tear at the world of convention is to try to strip the suffocating mask off the face of nature. What men call "good" is false and constricting; it has to be overthrown. As De Beauvoir says:

> It was not by chance that he [Sade] chose Easter as the day to whip Rose Keller, and it was at the moment that he sardonically suggested that he confess her that his sexual excitement reached its climax. No aphrodisiac is so potent as defiance of the Good (*Ibid.*, p. 40).

In this way, the sadist is liberated from the inhibitions and the hypocrisy of social meanings. We are all prone to this kind of liberation, which is why we enjoy cheating in small things and why adolescents, especially, like to steal. We are trying to affirm that our organism and our sense of self is somehow more vital and basic than the world of symbols, of do's and don't's, that has been grafted onto it. We all experience a catharsis when some areas of man-made meanings are desecrated. It may leave us weak and a bit nauseous, but it leaves us somewhat purified. In, say, a viewing of Luis Buñuel's *Viridiana* everyone in the audience is treated to a spectacle of the world being cut down to size. They are offered the possibility of a grandiosity that accompanies the leveling of all values. For this reason a motion picture that portrays the destruction of cultural values holds a strange fascination: it strips man of what is felt to be most basic in his life—the sense of the Good and the True. And this is why such a stripping is accompanied by extreme discomfort, even nausea, and the feeling of having been emptied and violated. A completely sadistic catharsis elevates the individual organism at the expense of the social world, but precisely in this elevation there is a violation of his basic social

nature. Hence the secret attraction of sadism and its simultane-
ous repugnance. Modern man is not as wise as some of the
primitive tribes who had special rituals during which the
whole tribe was given license to defy the gods and the most
sacred beliefs. It was an exercise in ritualized sadism, an "in-
stitutionalized" catharsis. Modern man is not so fortunate, and
has to contrive his defiances in petty, lonely, and ingenious
ways: and so in order to understand his efforts, we need to
invent a psychiatric category instead of a ritual-religious one.

The Ontological Aspect

The value aspect of sadism is thus easy enough to understand; but it depends on another dimension which is more
difficult to convey—what we might call the ontological aspect
of sadism. As we can see from the above examples, when man
defies cultural conventions he defies them in the name of a
higher, more basic, more vital truth—Nature, as for Sade; the
living people, as for some primitives; the potential of Man,
as for Nietzsche; and so on. In sadism, man is opposing the
vital and the living to the stilted, the abstract, and the dead. He
is opposing the pulsating organism to the ghostly symbol, the
embodiment of the life force to the schematic rules and codes
that constrain it.

This opposition between thought and things goes very
deeply into human experience. And in order to understand
what the sadist is trying to do when he tortures another's body,
we have to understand this duality. So let us dwell on it for a
moment. All organisms have two dimensions—an inside and an

[26]

outside. And all organisms who deal with other organisms, who confront them in nature and in life, have to be able to react to these dimensions. Lower animals mostly have to deal only with the external aspects of the objects they meet; they react to color, size, smell, and movement. But man has a special burden: he has to pay great attention to the possible meanings concealed in the insides of organismic objects. We live in two kinds of space: we occupy external space with our organic bodies, and we possess an internal space that seems to be occupied by an indwelling consciousness. As James Mark Baldwin, one of the principal early theorists on this problem, put it: "I can get at others' minds only through their bodies; I read a physical series straight up to a psychic terminus, whenever I discover my friend's emotion . . ." (1906, p. 259). Thus man is burdened with the need to be sensitive to two ranges of organismic experience, whereas the lower animals have only one: the open, public, organic aspect of things. Yet even among apes and dogs we already seem to detect a sensitivity to the private, inner, personal aspect of experience, to the conscious inner intent of organisms: an ape can assume a menacing posture, a charged stance, a swagger, which induces others to give him a wide berth. In man this sensitivity is carried to an extreme, and the history of a human life is largely a learning to disregard the outer appearances of human objects, and to try to divine inner intentions. Man, unlike lower animals, has a minimum of external cues to what others will be like, and he lacks instinctive responses to the intentions of people he meets; so he has to be extra alert to what they might be thinking or planning, deep down inside. But we are not equally skilled at hiding our own inner intentions, or reading those of others, and so folk wisdom talks about the advantages of a "poker face" and the reliability of "woman's intuition."

If people are not equally skilled in reckoning with this double range of experience, we would expect one important corollary: namely, that *each and every human being would have a preference for transacting with one or the other aspect of the reality of his object—inner or outer.* And we would further expect that in certain individuals this preference would be so extreme that one or the other aspect of the reality of his objects—inner or outer—would be a positive threat to him; he would not have dependable behavior patterns for dealing with this aspect of persons. So we would find some people who prefer objects that are primarily external and physical; others would seek out objects that are primarily internal and mental. Or put another way, some of us would prefer to relate to the outside of people's bodies; others, to the insides. A workingman cannot be comfortable with what the consciousness of an intellectual represents; he has no way of coping with it. He prefers an organism with rough hands, and one who can hold a lot of whiskey. He cannot go far beyond the body. A sensitive intellectual, on the other hand, sees no value in a rough exterior, and cannot deal with a shallow interiority; he is literally stopped dead, has nothing to take hold of.

These homely examples help us to stress, finally, a most important thing: that in our feeling for what is *real,* some of us would grant greater status, higher existential priority, to the natural organic aspects of things; others among us would grant this status only to the cultural-symbolic aspects of things. We would invest human objects with meaning in a lopsided way; we would devalue one or another aspect of human reality.[3]

And now we are in a position to understand that when someone like Sade hated convention because it worked against nature, he would also *scorn thought processes* because they were not as *real* as *bodies*. Indwelling consciousness, for such a man, would have a false integrity, it would lack tangibleness and genuineness, it would be too separate and aloof from the world of things. The great moment for the sadist, then, would be precisely when he could "get at" others' minds—to use Baldwin's expression; when he could treat them with the scorn they deserve. And the only way to do this is "through their bodies." By treating the flesh with violence and causing it great pain, the sadist literally makes of his partner a *predominantly external organism:* there is no room for the subtleties of thought, and no way of keeping thought separate from what one feels and expresses, when he is convulsed with pain. The mind "comes out in the open" in the screams and pleadings of the body. There is no longer anything private or aloof: the victim is reduced to the barest terms of the body; all indwelling values, all cultivated sensitivity, all the graceful forms of thought and talent, all that man earns and learns as a cultural animal are reduced whimperingly and totally to the terms of the tortured flesh. When the sadist torturer "breaks" his victim he means that he has been able to bring the inner self of the other to full view and control. Simone de Beauvoir aptly notes the supreme delight with which the sadist contemplates "the exceptional moment in which a lucid mind inhabits a body which is being degraded into matter" (1953, pp. 41–42). This is the "radical transformation" that the sadist seeks: to convert the domain of symbols into the hard currency of matter. The ultimate orgiastic satisfaction is achieved when all the barriers are broken down, when everything that was formerly threateningly and unnaturally apart melts into an esthetic whole.

Sado-masochism as Weakness

And so we may understand how the sadistic experience can be a totally liberating one: it represents a mastery over two dimensions of human experience that seem artificial and antinatural: the social motives that cause inhibitions, and the private symbolic meanings that are a reservoir of duplicity. The sadist takes the value aspect of the human reality and the ontological inner aspect, and lumps them together in the flesh for all to see. He wants to affirm what is most basic as he understands the world; he seems to be wanting to say: "The physical and the natural alone have value." We began these few pages of our discussion of sado-masochism by noting this in order to show how different the perversions of the adult may be from those of the child. But now we run the risk of glamorizing the sadist, of making him seem truly talented, a special servant of human liberation from all that is debasing and constricting. Yet we know this is not so: by violating persons and by scorning the best of man's symbolic achievements, the sadist is himself the debaser. If the sadist resembles an artist in the service of human freedom, he is at best one who has gone astray, or at least one who is extremely limited in talent and creative talent. If his motives are more complex, in his rearrangement of the world, than the child's, his strength is no greater—and it is this that signals his own basic "perversion."

The fact is that the sadist is not adequate to the world, and this lies behind his intent to cut it down to manageable size. Stendhal noted long ago the sadist's basic insecurity:

> There are some men who are the victims and instruments of a hellish pride . . . These men, who are cruel perhaps because like Nero they are always afraid, judge everyone after their own pattern, and can achieve physical pleasure only when they indulge their pride by practising cruelties upon the companion of their pleasures. Hence the horrors of *Justine* [Sade]. Only in this way can they find a sense of security (1822, p. 26).

It is in his basic insecurity, in his inability to relate to total persons, that the sadist makes common cause with the fetishist. He seems to be saying: "*This* is the best way to take hold of the real, to bring myself into the world. By relating to the object in this way, my behaviors are adequate to the task of ultimate satisfaction." The fetishist is afraid of the other's total body, and can relate only to a part. The sadist is not afraid of the body, but of the insides, the privacy, the hard-earned individuality that does not show itself in the flesh; this is the "difference" he cannot stand: the mysteriousness of the object, its separateness, its uniqueness. Like the fetishist, he cannot relate to the world on *its* terms; we might say that what makes him uncomfortable is the multiplicity of the world, the manifoldness of private selves in it. It is this that places it beyond his sure powers. We all want to know what others have inside (see Nuttin's excellent article, 1950), but many of us can stand not knowing, if knowing means threatening the integrity of the other person. But this is precisely what the sadist cannot do: he seems to suffer from an exaggerated sensitivity to the artificial difference between insides and outsides of objects. Médard Boss noted this in one of his excellent case studies (1949). If he cannot relate to his partner as a whole, the sadist reduces him to a body, and will permit him to be nothing more.

This is where the difference between strong persons and weak or "perverted" ones comes to a head. Most of us like to deal with people who are unique, who seem to conceal an inner person which holds itself aloof from our best efforts at probing. This is the way we give life its abundance of meaning: we revel in the multiplicity of natural mystery. This is why we called the sadist an artist limited in talent or gone astray: he wants to affirm something more vital and natural than that which appears in the dealings of men. But in violating the privateness of others, he is accomplishing the very opposite result: he is depriving the human world of its one great source of vitality and mystery—the subjective depth of persons. And he does this, as we said, because this depth is a threat to his own limited powers, to his own weak sense of self. The sadist defeats genuine artistry by reducing everything to sameness; he denies higher powers by reducing everything to his own limited powers. True maturity for the individual resides in accepting self-transcendence; this is what gives life richer meaning. If, say, we worship the sun and thereby feel our privileged place in the vast panorama of creation, we are in effect glorifying ourselves, even while we appear to make ourselves subordinate. Sade was made miserable at the thought that even were he able to tear the sun out of the heavens, it would still make no difference to nature. The moral of this lament is that it takes strength to allow oneself to feel transcended.

The curse on the sadist is that he cannot accept the world on its terms, but that, nevertheless, he has to transact with its objects. Being a man, he is condemned to live in the world of men, with whatever interhuman talents he has. He has to deal with the world on its terms, and being powerless to grant it a measure of superordinate, private meaning which is not amenable to his behaviors, he must tear at it senselessly and clumsily. Simone de Beauvoir has understood this about Sade, and notes that "had he been cold by nature, no problem would ever have arisen; but his instincts drove him toward outside objects with which he was incapable of uniting, so that he was forced to invent singular methods for taking them by force" (1953, p. 33). Incapable, that is, in terms that we have outlined here, possessing a too narrow range of accommodative behaviors. The sadist "shrinks from the kind of equality which is created by mutual pleasure" (*Ibid.*, p. 33). The point here is that it takes strength to be equal, to allow the object *to make a claim on you* on its own terms.[4]

This is perhaps the final moral of our remarks: that the person who lacks such strength is the one who really worships *force.* This is why the hyphen is justified in the word sado-masochism, why the two are usually found together: the impoverished person is the one who feels that anything that *can be affirmed forcefully* has value. Whether he is the one who inflicts pain or the one who suffers it, by using and submitting to force he comes under the dominion of the really real, the natural and vital. The weaker we are, the more limited is our action, but necessarily the greater is the forceful commitment with which we undertake it.

And so we may conclude that the "perversions" of our private worlds are not matters for medical psychiatry, but are questions of social learning. Man has no "instincts" to renounce in order to become human; he becomes human by developing powers commensurate with responsible social living, by learning to endure failure, by respecting the integrity of other humans, by sagaciously testing the limits of his claims, by being suspicious of force, and seeking to check its use and dominion among men.

So, too, the perversions of our national life are not matters of politics, of the frantic fetishization of force embodied in military and police power. Rather, they too are matters of educating a strong, independent, self-reliant people, who will be happy and patient to live with threatening complexity and overwhelming mystery. As writers through the ages have urged, man becomes supremely man by cultivating a sense of tragedy, responsibility, and awe. Our planet still waits in vain for the birth of such a people.

SUMMER, 1962

Notes

1. See the excellent document, "Feelings of a Fetishist," by "Boots" (pseudonym), *Psychiatric Quarterly*, Vol. 31 (1957), pp. 742–58.

2. Thus, the frequent search for extra dimensions of the fetish object, like smell. The fetishist seems to be seeking some kind of vicarious contamination of the object by its former human occupant; this is a contamination that broadens the range of the fetish object's meaning by relating it to something beyond itself. This would not represent a "repressed coprophillic desire" (Karl Abraham, "Remarks on the Psycho-analysis of a Case of Foot and Corset Fetishism," in *Selected Papers on Psychoanalysis*, London: Hogarth, 1948) but rather an attempted broadening out of stimulation from the narrow object itself. The fetishist, let it be continually stressed, is creative *from within* his behavioral poverty, rather than heaped up with repressed instincts.

3. So, we include in the study of characterology, "thought-valuing" and "thing-valuing" individuals. The early characterology, especially of the beginning of this century, dealt very subtly with these dimensions. Now that we are in the post-Freudian epoch, one can predict that this work will be revived and will come fully into its own. I am thinking especially of the greatness of a work like Eduard Spranger's *Types of Men*, an approach that should never have been eclipsed by Freudianism and by medical psychiatry, but should have been amalgamated theoretically with them. Perhaps the main value, historically, of existential phenomenology, will be to turn us back to the earlier characterology, especially of Dilthey's school. The interested student should consult A. A. Roback's important book, *The Psychology of Character*.

4. This, of course, is an ideal enjoinder since such strength is very rare. That is why we are all sadists to a certain extent, at least at certain times. And this is not only because we may lack strength to support all kinds of meanings; it is also because we need to protect the legitimacy of the meanings we already share: we need to deny that the social drama is symbolic and fictional, not "given" in nature, but somehow contrived by man. Take, for example, the individual in our group who puts forth a claim to an identity that we do not think justified. Say, the school chum who suddenly returns from college with a newly developed British accent. Why do his friends needle him sadistically? Simply because they are reluctant to accept fabricated values that are not grounded in *earned experience*. We might accept a person's right to assume a British accent if we were assured that he had "spent a few years" studying in Britain. The difference is that these few years serve to "anchor" the symbols in the lived organismic experience—which alone gives them some kind of legitimacy. So, too, we share the sadist's world view when we make this protest, since we affirm that lived justification can only be had basically in flesh-experience; we feel that only the tangible is real, the symbolic is sham. We are threatened by symbolic values that are capable of being turned on and off at will, since this tends to reveal that all cultural values are capable of being assumed, and are thus basically fictional.

References

Allen, Frederick H. (1937), "The Dilemma of Growth," *Archives of Neurology and Psychiatry,* Vol. 37, pp. 857–67.
———— (1940), "Homosexuality in Relation to the Problem of Human Difference," *American Journal of Orthopsychiatry,* Vol. 10, pp. 129–35.
Baldwin, James Mark (1906), *Thought and Things,* Vol. 1, *Functional Logic, or Genetic Theory of Knowledge* (London: Swan Sonnenschein).
Beauvoir, Simone de (1953), *The Marquis de Sade* (New York: Grove Press).
Becker, E. (1964), *The Revolution in Psychiatry: The New Understanding of Man* (New York: Free Press).
Boss, Médard (1949), *Meaning and Content of Sexual Perversions: A Daseinsanalytic Approach to the Psychopathology of the Phenomenon of Love,* Liese Lewis Abell (trans.) (New York: Grune and Stratton, 2nd edition).
Fourier, Charles (1849), quoted in Frank Manuel, *The Prophets of Paris* (Cambridge: Harvard University Press, 1962).
Goldfarb, William (1961), *Childhood Schizophrenia* (Cambridge, Massachusetts: The Commonwealth Fund).
Goodman, Paul (1962), *Utopian Essays and Practical Proposals* (New York: Random House).
Nagler, Simon (1957), "Fetishism: A Review and a Case Study," *Psychiatric Quarterly,* Vol. 31, pp. 713–41.
Nuttin, Josef (1950), "Intimacy and Shame in the Dynamic Structure of Personality," in M. L. Reymert (ed.), *Feelings and Emotions* (New York: McGraw-Hill), pp. 343–52.
Sartre, Jean-Paul (1956), *Being and Nothingness* (New York: Philosophical Library).

Stendhal (1822), *Love,* Gilbert and Suzanne Sale (trans.) (London: The Merlin Press, 1957).

Whitehead, Alfred N. (1958), *Modes of Thought* (New York: Capricorn Books).

Wolpe, J. and Rachman, S. (1960), "Psychoanalytic 'Evidence': A Critique Based on Freud's Case of Little Hans," *Journal of Nervous and Mental Disease,* Vol. 131, pp. 135–48.

II | KAFKA ON THE OEDIPUS COMPLEX

An Essay for S.

Franz Kafka knew . . . [Freud's] theories very well and considered them always as a very rough and ready explanation which didn't do justice to detail, or rather to the real heartbeat of the conflict.

MAX BROD *(Franz Kafka: A Biography)*

For me you took on the enigmatic quality that all tyrants have whose rights are based on their person and not on reason.

FRANZ KAFKA *(Letter to His Father)*

Franz Kafka's short story "The Judgment: a Story for F." must surely rank as one of the great self-analytic documents in the whole history of human reflection. It may well be the greatest, if we judge it by the wealth of insight woven with the highest artistry into the briefest space. This interweaving literally leaves the informed student breathless. From the little literature that I know, the only self-analytic writings that even approach it are Thomas Traherne's *Centuries of Meditations,* the "Third Century," and perhaps a few of Herman Melville's short stories. Kafka's story, as we shall see, is about a typical Oedipus complex, *almost* in the classic Freudian sense; yet, with a breadth, depth, and subtlety which would have surprised and taught even Freud. It shows that Kafka had no superior in his understanding of the situation of the child in relation to his parents. As a psychologist he must rank with Freud and Kierkegaard. He could be dispassionately analytic as they were—as in his great confession "Letter to His Father"; or he could be emotional and artistic and offer up his deepest self-analytic insights.

Kafka's story, then, has a truly great educative potential for us, if we can reveal its artistic and emotional meaning by means of a clear intellectual analysis. When we can put rational closure on emotional, artistic intuition, we achieve the perfect learning experience; we lay bare the human condition in complete roundness—both as felt and as thought. And this is the experience I propose to the reader. Let me at the outset apologize humbly for the ease with which I try to make clear intellectual capital out of Kafka's legacy in this story. There is a certain scavenging in such an undertaking, which the "man of knowledge" cannot deny. After all, he earns his respectability and his imposing title in a somewhat "dishonest" way: he is not fully involved as a person with his subject matter; if he masters it, it is with grace and ease, with the sly shiftiness of symbols, there where the artist literally squeezed his insights out of his own flesh, blood, and bones, and expired young because of the effort. Freud, who got many things backward, thought it was just the other way around: he once remarked—almost pompously—that the scientist has to work so hard to get the insights that the writer tosses off so easily. And this is the hubris of the scholar, who becomes imposingly gray at the temples, rummaging around and putting order into the anguished insights of tormented youth who leave behind the distillation of their genius and collapse early into their graves. Especially is this characterization true of Kafka's life and his document, which not only lays bare the pathetic human condition, but also must reveal Kafka's own anguish. Let us then approach it with proper respect, and some fear and trembling, and let us follow our teacher reverently.

The story[1] covers a short period of a Sunday morning in spring; its two main characters are George Bendemann, a young merchant, and his aging father, whose business he helps run. It takes place in their home, where they live alone since the death of George's mother. The story begins with George dreamily gazing out of the window, thinking about his friend in St. Petersburg, to whom he has just penned a letter.

For the first few pages of the story, George etches a portrait of his friend as someone who was not succeeding in business in St. Petersburg. He would like to ask him to come home, but this is a touchy matter, this giving of advice to a prodigal by his home-body friend. How would he take the advice? Could one even be sure that this advice was the correct one? Decidedly, one had to go easy with the sensitivities of others, especially one's friends. All the more so, since in the three years since his friend's departure, George had applied himself with great determination to his father's business, and had done extremely well: the staff had doubled, and the turnover was five times as great as previously. All this had happened in the two years since George's mother's death. Had his father become less aggressive since that tragic time, and allowed George to develop his own business skills? Or was it merely a matter of good fortune? Probably the latter, mused George. Anyway, his friend had no inkling of this improvement, and George shrank from lording his newly won success over his absent friend.

So George's letters were confined to unimportant gossip, including the mention of an engagement by an unimportant man to an unimportant girl. Perhaps his friend had guessed that in this oblique way George was announcing his own engagement, and he began to show interest in this event. If George hadn't talked with his friend about Fraülein Frieda Brandenfeld, he often discussed his friend with her, and the peculiar turn that their relationship had taken in their correspondence. It gave rise to the following dialogue:

> "So he won't be coming to our wedding," said she, "and yet I have a right to get to know all your friends." "I don't want to trouble him," answered George, "don't misunderstand me, he would probably come, at least I think so, but he would feel that his hand had been forced and he would be hurt, perhaps he would envy me and certainly he'd be discontented and without being able to do anything about his discontent he'd have to go away again alone. Alone—do you know what that means?" "Yes, but may he not hear about our wedding in some other fashion?" "I can't prevent that, of course, but it's unlikely, considering the way he lives."

With these few lines of dialogue, Kafka concludes his excellent miniature portrait of an indecisive young man, self-effacing, obviously subordinate to the friend he so much admires. George's fiancée, sensing this contrast between his timidity and the superordinacy of the friend that George has injected into their relationship, has a flash of insight about the man she is about to marry, and says:

"Since your friends are like that, George, you shouldn't
ever have got engaged at all."

She means, of course, that since George has so little courage
vis-à-vis his friends, he is not the type to marry at all. But
George is no longer alone in this, since he obliged her to share
his relationships; and so he can absolve himself with a certain
decisiveness:

"Well, we're both to blame for that; but I wouldn't have
it any other way now."

But she soon has it her way as she draws her own relationship around him with kisses, and claims she feels upset. George
decides that "it could not really involve him in trouble were
he to send the news to his friend." Note Kafka's choice of
thoughts for his squeamish hero. George arrogates to himself
a mock courage, and an undeserved decisiveness, with these
lines that close the paragraph:

"That's the kind of man I am and he'll just have to take
me as I am," he said to himself. "I can't cut myself to another
pattern that might make a more suitable friend for him."

The lie is quickly revealed in the next paragraph, as he indeed
does write to his friend, as he promised Frieda, but in a most
self-effacing way, carefully suggesting that his forthcoming
marriage in no way weakens their friendship. It is almost as
though he were marrying to please his friend.

And so what is really the brief introduction to the story
closes on this portrait of George, and we move to the main
business, the interaction of this wispy character, George, with
his father. It begins with George going to his father's room,

where he had not been for months. The reason he has not been there is important for the subsequent action: he sees his father daily at business, but it is hinted that he has perhaps been neglecting his father for his fiancée. The father's room is dark, and one corner is hung with mementos of George's dead mother. The father rises to meet George, and we sense a bit of the fantastic in his figure as his "heavy dressing-gown swung open as he walked and the skirts of it fluttered round him." George's first impression is important because it confirms the fantasy of his perception of his father: "My father is still a giant of a man," said George to himself. I say "fantasy," because we shall shortly see how easily George carries this "giant" in his arms like a baby.

He tells his father in a vacant way that he has just sent news of his engagement to his friend in St. Petersburg; and almost as if to confirm the fact, he draws the letter a little way out of his pocket. It seems like a little enough matter, but immediately we sense something awry: what should be a simple and mundane communication takes on sudden overtones of a confrontation:

"To St. Petersburg?" asked his father.
"To my friend there," said George trying to meet his father's eye. In business hours he's quite different, he was thinking, how solidly he sits here with his arms crossed.

With this observation, it is obvious that George senses the confrontation. Why are things different during business hours? Perhaps because there George is on his own, more than a peer. At home he is again in a minus position, having to justify himself to his parent. Thus the increased solidity of the father.

"Oh yes. To your friend," said his father, with peculiar emphasis.

The peculiar emphasis heightens the confrontation: what does it mean? George must sense this, because his answer can only be read at the tempo of a nervous babble, an attempt at self-justification. No sooner finished with this attempt than his father presses the point, heightens his own solidity as an adversary:

"And now you've changed your mind?" asked his father, laying his enormous newspaper on the window-sill and on top of it his spectacles, which he covered with one hand.

Note the adjective enormous, and the decisive laying on the hand, which further intimidates George to further nervous and circuitous self-justification. And with his father's answer, the real confrontation begins, and the story takes its first sudden and unexpected turn (I have italicized the significant words and phrases):

"George," said his father lengthening his *toothless mouth,* "listen to me! You've come to me about this business, to talk it over with me. No doubt that does you honour. But it's nothing, it's worse than nothing, if you don't tell me the whole truth. I don't want to stir up matters that shouldn't be mentioned. Since the death of *our dear mother* certain things have been done that aren't right. Maybe the time will come for mentioning them, and maybe sooner than we think. There's many a thing in the business I'm not aware of, maybe it's not done behind my back—I'm not going to say that it's done behind my back—I'm not equal to things any longer, my memory's failing, I haven't an eye for so many things any longer. That's *the curse of Nature* in the first place, and in the second place the death of *our dear mother* hit me harder than it did you—but since we're talking about it, about this letter, I beg you George, don't deceive me. It's a trivial affair, it's hardly worth mentioning, so don't deceive me."

And then, like an explosion:

"Do you really have this friend in St. Petersburg?"

In order to understand what follows—George's immediate abject surrender in the face of these few words—we have to pause and see what has happened, what his father's words really mean to him. And here we must begin an exploration of the psychology of the parent-child relationship. The first thing to note is that his father lengthens his "toothless mouth." It is not the only time that Kafka gives us a striking concrete image; they recur at strategic points all through the story and we will note them—we already noted how he laid his hand on the newspaper. This particular concrete image is not as important as subsequent ones, indeed, they are cumulative in their effect. But by his deliberate use of them, Kafka reveals how much he knows about one of the most basic aspects of the Oedipus complex. I mean the fact that one of the greatest and most immediate sources of the parent's power over the child lies in the historical and existential priority of the parent's *organism*. In the world of the child, the parent's *body* looms as a primary unexplainable miracle. *Things* are fantastic enough to the child—lights and birds and dogs and trees; but even more so are parents, whose voice begins in the child's own bowels, and rumbles through them as he sits on the parent's lap; parents, who existed from time immemorial, and who shall never die; parents, who are wise beyond belief, in whose slightest actions there may lurk clues to survival and greater well being for the child—perhaps in the blink of the eye, or the twitch of the cheek. And what does a moustache mean? How wonderful and mysterious it is.[2]

This marvel of the concrete parental organism is conveyed long before the child gets clear about the words that he learns from the parent: the words that make the commands so unmistakably pointed and constricting; the words that make him so dependent upon the parent, because they in turn give *him* symbolic power over things. The reaction of the child to the parent's *organism* is more primitive, and for that, more binding and overpowering. It is very much the pristine reaction of one animal to another: there is no way to render *the other presence* objective; it is unmanageable.

As far as I can see, this is the basic source and the meaning of *guilt* in the parent-child relationship; especially what the psychoanalysts refer to clumsily but truly as "unconscious guilt." As I have discussed it elsewhere,[3] guilt means that one's action is bound, that one is inhibited by an object *without knowing why*. And the most direct and unfathomable source of such inhibition is the existential priority and awesomeness of the concrete parental organism. It is this superordinacy of the parent that takes root well before the child learns symbols: hence it is not subject to conscious scrutiny (therefore it is "unconscious"). Furthermore—and this is important—even if the miraculousness of the parental organism *were* subject to symbolic scrutiny, there would still be no way of *explaining* the primary miracle of the created organism. Hence, this is a *natural* and *symbolically unresolvable guilt,* that is, a deep feeling that one's own existence is hopelessly transcended by the priority of all of creation: If we open our sensitivities to the majesty and miracle of creation, then we must "truly" crumble to our knees in palpitating fear and smallness, and in some kind of gratitude for having been given the transient "privilege" of *just being a spectator.* This is what the existential phenomenologists mean by "ontological" or "real" guilt, as opposed to "existential" or "circumstantial" guilt—the guilt that springs from our life history. But we can see that the two are inseparable: the transcendence of the parent's inhibiting commands are rooted in the ontological transcendence of his concrete organism. There is no way for the child, even growing into the most mature and reflective adult, to live down the injustice of the decay and death of the marvelous parental organism—because it *is* ontologically unjust. Even if the child could absolve himself of any part in the causing of this decay and death, still its injustice transcends and humbles him. It is this that gives him the irreducible feeling of being bound and beholden, that makes his surrender "natural."

In the light of these remarks, we can return to Kafka's story, and see just what George's father's words must have meant to him. We have not only the superordinacy of the father, but of both parents, of *"our* dear mother," even though dead—especially because dead: the twice repeated "our" of the parent takes unquestioned precedence over the selfish "I" of George. And it is not a matter of anyone's intention, it is *"the curse of*

Nature"—the ontological injustice that makes for the ineffaceable guilt! In the face of this, George's affairs, his involuted dealings with his friend, are trivial—as the father says; they are hardly worth mentioning. In fact, it is not even important that he has a friend or a personal life. And so his immediate and abject surrender—both of his friend and of his personal life. George rises in embarrassment and makes the fitting renunciation:

> "Never mind my friends. A thousand friends wouldn't make up to me for my father. Do you know *what I think?* You're not taking enough care of yourself. But old age must be taken care of. *I can't do without you in the business,* you know that very well, but if the business is going to undermine your health, *I'm ready to close it down* to-morrow for ever. And that won't do. *We'll have to make a change* in your way of living. But a radical change. You sit here in the dark, and in the sitting-room you would have plenty of light. You just take a bite of breakfast instead of properly keeping up your strength. You sit by a closed window, and the air would be so good for you. *No, Father!* I'll get the doctor to come, and we'll follow his orders. We'll change your room; you can move into the front room and I'll move in here. You won't notice the change, all your things will be moved with you. But there's time for all that later, I'll put you to bed now for a little, I'm sure you need to rest. Come, I'll help you to take off your things, you'll see I can do it . . .

There are two shocking things about this paragraph (of which I have omitted only the last two sentences, repetitive of the main theme), both of which need explaining. The first, George's surrender, we have already dealt with. The second thing is a function of it, but is just as shocking: I mean the brand new decisiveness of George, the sudden emergence of a firm personality, conveyed by the lines I put in italics, and carried on all through the paragraph. What are we to make of this new firmness and command?

The answer, of course, is that it is a delegated power, the authority of a slave in the service of a lordly master. This sudden switch to the complete masochistic posture is the *only role* available to George, after he was negated as a person in the confrontation with his father. What does one do in the face of a self-negating source of power? He must either triumph over it, or bend to it; find his identity by defeating it, or serving it; and George accepts to serve—it is the only alternative available to him. He even possibly lies to keep this new identity integral, as he tells his father he cannot do without him in the business: earlier he had allowed himself to think that one of the possible reasons the business was thriving is that his father had given him a freer hand. Now he suppresses that thought entirely. He will be the perfectly self-effacing servant, even to forfeiting his own room. In the next few lines, Kafka drives home the superordinacy of the father, with more images of his organismic concreteness (my emphasis):

> George stood close beside his father, who had let his *head* with its *unkempt white hair sink on his chest.*
> "George," said his father in a low voice, *without moving.*

The impression of solid power is crushing to George, who immediately goes down on his knees beside his father. And in the next phrase Kafka makes the concrete suggest the fantastic:

. . . in the old man's weary face he saw the pupils, over-large, fixedly looking at him from the corners of the eyes.

We feel the chilling quality of George's perceptions, the fantastic of the concrete object. After all, there is no decisive line that can be drawn around the awesomeness of the primary miracle of the created concrete object: it exudes the fantastic.

The next paragraph brings a slight relief and change of pace: George's father opens up the possibility of a rational discussion about George's friend, and with this new possibility, the stifling power of the father is temporarily lifted. He says:

"You have no friend in St. Petersburg. You've always been a leg-puller and you haven't even shrunk from pulling my leg. How could you have a friend out there! I can't believe it."

By saying "I can't believe it," instead of categorically denying it as he did earlier, he leaves an opening for possible discussion, for the fresh air of objective fact. Not only does George rise to it, but it also helps reveal the father in a more objective light. As George says "Just think back a bit, Father," he lifts his father from the chair and slips off his dressing gown, as the old man "stood feebly enough"! In other words, the real father is not the "giant of a man" that George earlier saw, but a feeble one who can actually be lifted. We will see further how Kafka alternates these real perceptions of fact with George's own distorted perceptions; nor can we afford to overlook them since the whole artistry of the story is carried in this duality of perception, and it reveals the story's true meaning and sense. The Oedipus complex, after all is said and done about it, really conveys one thing: the fact that the child's perceptions of the world are shaped and distorted by his early training. He never gets a true estimate of himself, or a true evaluation of reality in terms of his own powers. And it is just this discrepancy in basic perception that Kafka is intent on relating here. George is dealing with a father who is largely a phantasm of his own imagination; and this phantasm is unleashed precisely because George's power of action and independent decision is curtailed by the parental relationship.

George reminds his father of his friend, how he came to visit at their home, and so on; and in this reminder we again read what a subordinate position George had in his own home, in relation to his father: how he twice kept his father from seeing his friend, although the friend was actually sitting in George's room. George even had to smuggle his friendships for fear of his father's disapproval.

In the next paragraph, George carries on in the role he has assumed—that of willing servant; he undresses his father, reproaching himself for the not-too-clean appearance of his underwear. He carries his father to bed in his arms, and as he does so, Kafka reveals to us two striking things in a very brief three-line paragraph.

> It gave him a dreadful feeling to notice that while he took the few steps towards the bed the old man on his breast was playing with his watch-chain. He could not lay him down on the bed for a moment, so firmly did he hang on to the watch-chain.

The image of the old man dangling on the watch string is a graphic reversal of the Oedipal situation: it is now the son who is the father to the babe, as the babe dangles on the watch chain. And this gives George a dreadful feeling. Dreadful, Kafka says, conveying the full Kierkegaardian anxiety. Where does the slave stand when he loses his master; when he loses the firm locus of superordinate authority on which the power of his being rests? In the void of dread, as both Kafka and Kierkegaard knew.

Let us linger on this for a moment because it is crucial to understanding the Oedipus complex in another of its basic dimensions. We mentioned above that the idea of the Oedipus complex conveys one thing above all: that the child's perceptions of the world are shaped and distorted by his early training—that he never gets a true estimate of reality in relationship to his unique and individual powers. This is one basic dimension of the Oedipus, and it suggests a necessary complementary dimension: I mean that if the child fails to get a true estimate of his powers, it must be because they are somehow curtailed and interfered with by other powers in the form of commands, prohibitions, forcible constraint, willful trickery, or even routine and innocuous cajoling and bribery. But the result is ineluctable: in some variety of ways, the child abrogates the full aegis over his own individuality, and comes to rely on outside powers and rules, in order to sustain and justify his very existence and his right to act. The result of this dependence on outside powers is at the root of most tyranny by man over men. People get the very mandate of their lives from power sources outside of them, from other concrete organisms who embody authority, from codes of conduct, from networks of symbols, from intricate proprieties of all types. So that these outside sources come to assume a *sanctity* for which the individual would willingly give his life since without them he feels and believes that he could not sustain his life anyway. Hence, he feels *dread* at precisely that point where superordinate authority risks fading away, being replaced, overthrown, or even outgrown. Freud himself conveyed personally this fundamental aspect of the Oedipus complex in one of his very last writings, when he understood that behind one of his neurotic troubles was his reluctance to surpass his father.[4] Small wonder, as we said, that man is the greatest tyrant over man; no sacrifice is too great to protect the authority in which one's life is rooted—and the authority which others defend is always "less valid" than the one we are championing: why, we feel it in our very blood and bones! "In our hearts"—as one recent aspirant to the United States Presidency put it—we know who is "right." And what better final arbiter over whose blood is to be spilled than the intuitions of one's heart? Alas, the thing that the masses of men must one day learn, if *Homo sapiens* is to survive, is that the pure heart in which they base their trust is itself the first thing sullied by the ways and personages of the world into which they are born.

In the next lines of dialogue, Kafka sets the stage for a step that he likes to take in his stories, a step from a real and plausible story into a frankly fantastic one. It is a step that is crucial to his message since it permits him to blur completely the line between real perception and fantasy perception and to show how inseparable they are. By taking his story into fantasy, he is able to show what is really at stake for George, and he is able to take all of his previous hints and painful insights, and open them to the size of full and hideous wounds. Thus, we are invited to see that George's Oedipus complex is not a mere confrontation with humiliating authority, not a simple maneuvering for identity, not a clever and circumspect game in which to salvage some kind of self-respect: rather, it purely and simply is a death sentence, the abrogation of one's right to live.

The break into fantasy occurs just after George tucks his father into bed, and seems reassured that in his new role as nursemaid he is tolerably good, that all now "seemed well." But his father seems strangely intent on an answer as to whether he is well covered up; and as George reassures him that he is well covered, the break into fantasy begins:

> "No!" cried his father, cutting short the answer, threw the blankets off with a strength that sent them all flying in a moment and sprang erect in bed. Only one hand lightly touched the ceiling to steady him.

The fantastic image is not only powerfully phallic, but in the new strength that the father now has, as well as in the perfect dexterity of his fingering of the ceiling, we know that we have left the world of reality. What we can expect now is a frank and brutal twisting of the real, and this is just what Kafka puts into the father's denunciation of George:

> "You wanted to cover me up, I know, my young sprig, but I'm far from being covered up yet. And even if this is the last strength I have, it's enough for you, too much for you."

George's inferiority, that Kafka merely suggested, now becomes explicit, both as regards the father and the friend.

The father continues:

> "Of course I know your friend. He would have been a son after my own heart. That's why you've been playing him false all these years. Why else?"

Here Kafka may be suggesting a real gulf in understanding between a strong father and a schizoid son: "Why else" would anyone have an inauthentic relationship to a friend, unless he was being false? The father cannot understand inauthenticity that stems from hypersensitivity and weakness—as most people cannot. So he suggests "falseness" and expresses his preference for the "genuine" son.

The father seems to be expressing the ambivalent bind that most parents are in: they prefer a strong and direct offspring, one who, by his presence, conveys a firmness and genuineness that brings more conviction into their lives.[5] But the ambivalence comes in in the fact that while most parents prefer such a strength and directness, they actually cannot handle it, and may even fear it: thus they themselves, as did George's father, create a timorous slave. This seems to be well borne out by the very next accusation by the father, where he reproaches the son for having assumed some independence and power in the family business:

> "Do you think I haven't been sorry for him? And that's why you had to lock yourself up in your office—the Chief is busy, mustn't be disturbed—just so that you could write your lying little letters to Russia."

He strips George of the right to independence and privacy in the business by suggesting that he uses it for his own petty purposes. Then the accusation becomes truly fantastic:

> "But thank goodness a father doesn't need to be taught how to see through his son. And now that you thought you'd got him down, so far down that you could set your bottom on him and sit on him and he wouldn't move, then my fine son makes up his mind to get married!"

There is no real relationship between this accusation and George's motives, we know it from the whole picture we have of George thus far; but George is overcome by it. He thinks of his friend with a surge of sympathy and heart-rending yearning. It is obvious that he is reaching out to his friend for support, in the face of his father's devastating negation of him:

> Why did he have to go so far away!

But George's mental casting about in the wastes of Russia, for a friend to come to his aid, is of no avail. The father is in command here:

> "But attend to me!" cried his father, and George, almost distracted, ran towards the bed to take everything in, yet came to a stop half-way.
> "Because she lifted up her skirts," his father began to flute, "because she lifted her skirts like this, the nasty creature," and mimicking her he lifted his shirt so high that one could *see the scar on his thigh from his war wound.*

I emphasize this last phrase to remind the reader of one of Kafka's main devices for portraying the superordinacy of the father in George's perception of him. As we saw earlier, by

stressing the *concreteness* of the physical organism, he completely cripples George's ability to cope with the father: guilt,
as we said, is the dumb inhibition one feels, as he is over-
shadowed by the existential concreteness of the parental organism. Here, Kafka carries this concreteness into another dimension, by showing not only its immediacy—the scar on the thigh
—but also by stressing the *superior historical career* of the
parental organism: the parent existed before the child, and had
the most marvelous experiences in a time that must seem
mythical precisely because one cannot rationally grasp it. In
our story, George is transcended by the reminder of heroism
in a war—a heroism and an experience that he obviously has
not duplicated in his own life.

But not only cannot George do this, he doesn't even have
the right to choose an honorable bride with honorable motives:
the bride is "nasty," and George's reason for marrying is itself
nasty:

> "because she lifted her skirts like this and this you made up
> to her, and in order to make free with her undisturbed you
> have disgraced your mother's memory, betrayed your friend
> and stuck your father into bed so that he can't move."

Again: not only the impugning of George's motives, the denial
of his right to private desires, but also the complete transcendence of his individuality, and its absorption in the superior
triad of mother, father, and friend. The father continues:

> "But he can move, or can't he?"
> And he stood up quite unsupported and kicked his legs out.
> His insight made him radiant.

The father is fantastic in his infallibility.

And just as we are about to feel matter of fact about the lopsided confrontation we are witnessing, just as our interest in George flags as it would about any *"pauvre type,"* Kafka draws us forward by letting in a draft of fresh air: we see another facet of George—the matter is not so cut and dried. Look here: Hard upon the fantasy perception of the radiant father Kafka juxtaposes a glimmer of real perception:

> George shrank into a corner, as far away from his father as possible. A long time ago he had firmly made up his mind to watch closely every least movement so that he should not be surprised by any indirect attack, a pounce from behind or above. At this moment he recalled this long-forgotten resolve and forgot it again, like a man drawing a short thread through the eye of a needle.

The thing is simply marvelous: what Kafka is telling us is that back in George's childhood he had the good sense to intuit that this man, his father, was actually his adversary, someone he had to watch in order not to be negated. Back in his past he was a potential individual, had sensed his right to have a self on his terms, and had resolved to be careful about achieving it. But what can a resolve like this mean for an animal who can only get his sense of self from his transactions with *others,* from *their* appraisal of *him?* Where is the individual to get the necessary purchase to expand his tiny island of self-feeling, in the face of a world which provides all the coin for that feeling —all the symbols, all the praise, all the organismic warmth and closeness, on which alone that feeling can be nourished and thrive? This is the Oedipal world. In such a world, one's sense of self is a fleeting feeling at best: to try to nourish it is indeed "like a man drawing a short thread through the eye of a needle."

Now again, the real perception is superseded by the fantastic one:

> "But your friend hasn't been betrayed after all!" cried his father, emphasising the point with stabs of his forefinger. "I've been representing him here on the spot."

Here the fantastic image is the stereotype of the lecturing father, and it gives itself away, invites undermining by reality. Besides, how could he be "representing" the friend? It is ridiculous. George rises to the task—and the fantasy image is in its turn superseded and attacked by another intuition about the reality. George blurts out:

> "You comedian!"

This is an absolutely new point in the dialogue; it is the first time that George has dared to phrase his fleeting intuitions into a direct denial of his adversary. And as we would expect, it is too heroic for George to sustain.

> George could not resist the retort, realized at once the harm done and, his eyes starting in his head, bit his tongue back, only too late, till the pain made his knees give.

He could not resist the retort because it was the pulse of his organism literally fighting for its existence. But the "harm" done? Here we must again harken back to our previous discussion: as we saw, the individual needs a superordinate source of power in which to ground his own existence. To negate that source is to negate oneself. One cannot let the light of reality into a situation in which one will himself be negated by that light. Hence, the "harm," and the terrible convulsive self-restraint of biting his tongue back till the pain made his knees give. Only such an image could convey the striking intuition that Kafka had: that the organism *literally fights against itself* in its urge toward freedom.

From the ejaculation "You comedian!," almost to the approaching end of the story, Kafka maintains this alternation between intuitions of reality and fantasy. George fights fleetingly for a foothold in the real, only to be resubmerged in the fantastic lie of the Oedipal situation.

Now the father:

> "Yes, of course I've been playing a comedy! . . . What other comfort was left to a *poor old widower?* Tell me—and while you're answering me be you still my living son—what else was left to me, in my back room, plagued by a disloyal staff, *old to the marrow of my bones?* And my son strutting through the world, finishing off deals that I had prepared for him, bursting with triumphant glee and stalking away from his father with the closed face of a respectable business-man! Do you think I couldn't have loved you, I, whom you turned your back on?"

Again, the superordinacy of the concrete physical organism, in the words I've italicized. And again the denial that George's own talent was in any way responsible for the recent upsurge in business. And again too, the final sentence which is so obviously untrue to George's real sentiments and actions that it allows him to see through the fantasy:

Now he'll lean forward, thought George; what if he topples and smashes himself! These words went hissing through his mind.

A puppet-comedian would indeed smash itself, but the idea "hisses" through George's mind for the same reasons that he earlier bit his tongue: the truth is unthinkable, and where thinkable, self-annihilating.

The father continues:

> "Stay where you are, I don't need you! You think you have enough strength to come over here and that you're only hanging back of your own accord. Don't be too sure! I am still much the stronger of us two. All by myself I might have had to give way, but your mother has given me so much of her strength that I've established a fine connection with your friend and I have your customers here in my pocket!"

Même jeu. Here the father fully denies George's autonomy over his own actions: George only *thinks* he can move or hang back of his own accord—but the father knows better. And once again the superordinacy of the father-mother team. The last sentence once more lets in the light of critical reality, since it is so ludicrous, and once again the fantastic alternates with the real but fleeting perception:

> "He has pockets even in his shirt!" said George to himself, and believed that with this remark he could make him an impossible figure for all the world. Only for a moment did he think so, since he kept on forgetting everything.

The short thread and the eye of the needle.

Now the father:

"Just take your bride on your arm and try getting in my way! I'll sweep her from your very side, you don't know how!"

The completely classical Oedipal threat: the son can never be the man his father is.

George made a grimace of disbelief. His father only nodded, confirming the truth of his words, towards George's corner.

In these two sentences, could Kafka have wanted to convey the ambivalence of the son in relationship to his own masculinity? I mean that the male can't really believe that he is not a male organism just like the father when he sees tangible proof in his appendages and beard and when everyone calls him "Mister." But he needs the confirmation of the father, because it is up to the father to support and to give the mandate for the *quality* of the son's maleness. If he doesn't do it, then that maleness is always in doubt.

The father continues:

"How you amused me to-day, coming to ask me if you should tell your friend about your engagement. He knows it all already, you stupid boy, he knows it all! I've been writing to him, for you forgot to take my writing things away from me. That's why he hasn't been here for years, he knows everything a hundred times better than you do yourself, in his left hand he crumples your letters unopened while in his right hand he holds up my letters to read through!"

In his enthusiasm he waved his arm over his head.

Once again the ludicrously exaggerated image invites the relief of a real perception:

"Ten thousand times!" said George, to make fun of his father, but in his very mouth the words turned into deadly earnest.

There is no way out for George, he must accept his father's version of truth; the sane observation is choked in his very mouth.

Now the father:

"For years I've been waiting for you to come with some such question! Do you think I concern myself with anything else? Do you think I read the newspapers? Look!" and he threw George a newspaper sheet which had somehow found its way into his bed. An old newspaper, with a name entirely unknown to George.

Here Kafka seems to be leading to George's final defeat: the paragraph is not relieved by a real perception on George's part —like the preceding two pages of dialogue. Furthermore it ends on a note of George's mystification in the face of the fantastic, rather than his usual glimmer of edification.

The father continues:

"How long a time you've taken to grow up! Your mother had to die, she couldn't see the happy day, your friend is going to pieces in Russia, even three years ago he was yellow enough to be thrown away, and as for me, you see what condition I'm in. You have eyes in your head for that!"

Once again, and finally, the superordinate trio of father, dead mother, and friend, and George now accused of the full guilt of their condition, of coming to manhood at their expense.

This is the knockout punch; it wrenches from George an anguished cry:

"So you've been lying in wait for me!"

With this cry he gives voice to the intuition he had had in his childhood: the resolve to be on guard against his father as the real adversary. But now in the desperation of his imminent defeat, he does not keep this resolve hidden—he blurts it out, confronts his father with it, and at the same time admits his defeat because he accepts his father's version of reality: He no longer attempts to pun the fantastic case built up by the father. It is now too late; he has lost; and the father confirms the defeat:

> His father said pityingly, in an off-hand manner: "I suppose you wanted to say that sooner. But now it doesn't matter."

(A perfectly true observation.)

> And in a louder voice: "So now you know what else there is in the world besides yourself, till now you've known only about yourself! An innocent child, yes, that you were, truly, but still more truly have you been a devilish human being!"

There is the case that the father has conjured up—there is no way for George to deny it. With all the "tricks" of the Oedipal superiority that the father has been able to marshal, he has rendered the fantastic real.

If the case is real, then the sentence is just and proper, and the father delivers it:

> "And therefore take note; I sentence you now to death by drowning!"

In other words, George's failure to overcome the Oedipal situation, his inability to get a consistently real perception of himself and his own powers, means that he has not been able to achieve integral personhood. Unable to overcome the false Oedipal perceptions, he has literally not been able to be born into manhood; and so, he must die. The step into fantasy that Kafka took a few pages back, when the father sprang up erect in bed, now has its symbolic culmination. The whole fantasy episode has served to lead up to the symbolic death sentence, which is the *real* judgment on George.

> George felt himself *urged* from the room, the crash with which his father fell on the bed behind him was still in his ears as he fled. On the staircase, which he *rushed down* as if the steps were an inclined plane, he ran into his charwoman on her way up to do the morning cleaning of the room. "Jesus!" she cried and covered her face with her apron, but he was already gone. Out of the front door he rushed, across the roadway, *driven* towards the water. Already he was *grasping* at the railings *as a starving man clutches food.*

We notice the compellingness of the death sentence in the words which I have put in italics: it is wholly out of George's power to resist: the parental *appraisal* of the child's personhood is itself a *command;* the parent's *opinions* become the child's *life-will.* It is terrifying. The charwoman seems already to have seen a living ghost.

Just as we reach the closing lines of the story, and are again about to relax with an open-and-shut case of a weakling son and a dominant and antagonistic father, Kafka once more stuns us with his genius:

> He swung himself over, like the distinguished gymnast he had once been in his youth, to his parents' pride.

Look there! The son is no weakling after all; and the parents were not his antagonists! In this remarkable sentence Kafka shows how well he has understood the Oedipus complex, and he invites us to ponder on what is really at stake in it. He is telling us nothing less than the fact that the symbolic death sentence pronounced on the person of George springs not from any *disapproval or differences* that the parents had with George; but rather from the fact that the son was willingly and lovingly embraced and ushered into their world view. And *this* is the deeper meaning of the Oedipus complex: it is the willing and helpless indoctrination, the benign approval, the ready embrace of the child who performs well in the fictional world of the family: it is this that *kills* his personhood, and not the competition for the female, the urge to a merely physical manhood in the face of a powerful father. These latter things are simply *ready symbols* for a much more pervasive undermining of the child's right to an independent existence. In other words, the whole fantastic episode of confrontation between George and his father was merely a symbol of a more subtle and pervasive defeat. A defeat by concord and compliance, by merging with instead of straining against, by being good instead of being bad.

What can one do in the face of such a defeat—how can one delineate antagonists among those who embrace you, who make your pride possible by giving you the love and approbation you need? Whom can one hate, and for what possible reason? There is no enemy where the victor who takes your life is the one who gave it to you in the first place, and nourished it into achievement. The only thing you can protest is your love: it is the only strong focus your emotions can take, the only clear direction in which your sense of self can expand. In sum, it is the only truth possible to you. George expresses it as he relinquishes his life with the same unobtrusiveness that he lived it:

> With weakening grip he was still holding on when he spied between the railings a motor-bus coming which would easily cover the noise of his fall, called in a low voice: "Dear parents, I have always loved you, all the same," and let himself drop.
>
> At this moment an unending stream of traffic was just going over the bridge.

AUGUST, 1967

Notes

1. I am using the translation from the German by Willa and Edwin Muir, in Franz Kafka, *The Penal Colony, Stories and Short Pieces,* New York: Schocken Books, 1948, pp. 49–63; British edition: *In the Penal Settlement, Tales and Short Prose Works,* London, Martin Secker and Warburg: 1949, pp. 45–59.

2. The great poet Thomas Traherne reminded us of things, in his own wonderful self-analytic revelations: see his *Centuries of Meditations,* especially the "Third Century."

3. *The Revolution in Psychiatry* (New York: Free Press, 1964).

4. "A Disturbance of Memory on the Acropolis," *Collected Papers,* Volume 5.

5. See some of my other writings on the problem of esthetics in human affairs for the theoretical background of this observation—especially *The Birth and Death of Meaning,* Chapter 8; *The Revolution in Psychiatry,* Chapter 8; *Beyond Alienation,* Chapter 8; and *The Structure of Evil,* Chapters 9 to 12.

III THE PAWNBROKER

A Study in Basic Psychology

[Unhappy are they] who struggle to be persons, not machines; to whom the Universe is not a warehouse, or at best a fancy-bazaar, but a mystic temple and hall of doom.

CARLYLE

Edward Lewis Wallant was another of those young geniuses—like Kafka—whose emotional and intuitive insight into the human condition was astonishing, and who literally squeezed this insight out of his own living flesh and consumed himself in the effort. Wallant died tragically early —in his middle thirties—but he had already proven himself a rare student of the character of man, and assured himself a place among the select few who can penetrate into the heart of the human condition. Consider the character delineations in such novels as *Children at the Gate,* or *The Pawnbroker.* Here is truly enormous penetration into what we might call "basic psychology": that is, the elemental psychic conditions for living and carrying on as *Homo sapiens* on this planet.

Here I want to discuss the film version of *The Pawnbroker,* which is a work of art in its own right, even though it takes some minor liberties with Wallant's story and a major liberty with the ending of it. I even venture the opinion that Morton Fine and David Friedkin's screen version created a more starkly realistic and integral study of character, even if it does not end on an ambiguous note of hope for the Pawnbroker as does Wallant's original story. I will try to show the basis for this judgment in the following pages. I think, too, that the screen version, with its bluntly tragic ending, makes a more "Christian" story rather than the "Judaic" one which Wallant intended, and my reason for holding this opinion will also be clear, I hope, to any student who might care to compare my brief analysis with Wallant's original story.[1] Parenthetically, I had delayed a long time in seeing the film because of the urging of so many people not to miss it: I prided myself on having learned that when so many different people are impressed, there is cause to be skeptical about finding a real work of art. Finally I went and saw that I was wrong: so many were impressed because there was literally "something for everyone": sex, violence, realism, Nazis and concentration camps, highly artful film-making, and superb acting—Rod Steiger at his best has no peer, and Sol Nazerman is surely his greatest role. But there was more, much more for the student of man; above all, as we said, there was psychology, elemental psychology, a dissection of man as a psychological being that was truly breathtaking in its cumulative force, and in the unfailing accuracy of its insight. The judgment is unmistakable: there are novelists and screenwriters who *know* man. The thing is all the more impressive in today's world because of the abundance of experts of all types—psychoanalysts, psychiatrists, clinical, experimental, and social psychologists—most of whom know only a fraction of what some professional writers know; and who, if they impress us at all, astonish us with the triviality and narrowness of their insight. *The Pawnbroker* shows man in depth and in the round, and this is its distinction in today's world of expert studies. Furthermore, *The Pawnbroker* reminds us of Kierkegaard's work for its understanding of the limits of the human condition, the point of no return. If there is one thing we are realizing in the present crisis in science, it is that we have to know all the dimensions of man's situation: not only what he is doing, but what he is most fervently trying to do, and what he cannot do by himself. Only in this direction lie the possibilities of growth and hope. And it is in this direction, if I am not mistaken, that *The Pawnbroker* feverishly points.

The film begins in as matter-of-fact way as possible: a backyard in suburbia, near New York City. A few people in the house voicing their daily cares and desires, and in a chair outside, a man, no longer young, and not quite there. It gradually becomes obvious that he is only physically in this world: his mind is continually prey to obtrusive flashbacks, flashbacks to a world he has left, but which still claims him. Physically and externally he is here; inwardly and emotionally he is elsewhere. But even his body is as burdensome as his memory: he seems to drag himself through the world as he goes about his daily business running a pawnshop in one of New York's ghettos. In itself, this burdensomeness of daily life is not enough to mark one harried New Yorker off from another. It becomes obvious that what really marks Nazerman off are those obtruding memories from a time past.

We soon learn what picture those memories compose, what the burden of his inner life is that makes his body so heavy and so tight. In a beautifully lilting slow-motion sequence we see a younger, gayer, more buoyant Nazerman picnicking in a field with his family somewhere in Poland. It must be the Sabbath. His two beautiful children—a girl and boy—are running in the tall grass, chasing butterflies. His very attractive wife watches the scene with quiet pride; and off to the side under a tree, his father wearing the traditional Jewish black skull cap, and reading—perhaps a prayer book. The whole scene, in lilting slow motion, is itself a prayer, a hymn to the God of Creation for the unspeakable beauty and bounty of life. Nazerman hefts his two children, one in each arm, and we sense what he feels; perfect plenitude, the tangible weight of a meaningful life, pressed up to his bosom. He literally breathes meaning, is immersed in it.

This flashback is silent, and we are caught up short by a sudden interruption: the people seem to hear a disquieting noise. In one terrible instant the whole hymn to Creation turns into the Dread of existence, as motorcycled Nazi troopers pull up to the field and take the family into custody. From here on Nazerman's story is one that my generation has lived vicariously so many times, we had rather be spared the details. We almost are—the thing is handled with such perfect economy: we see only a few heart-rending and soul-rending flashbacks. One is of the trip to the concentration camp in a cattle car, as Nazerman tries to hold his son up in the air to prevent him from slipping down into the mess of excrement from the two hundred degraded humans who press against each other and cannot move. The pleading face of his wife is of no avail, Nazerman can do nothing to prevent his son from slipping down; and the whole tone of the story is set as he shrieks his anguished helplessness in the face of his fate: "I am helpless, do you hear? I can do nothing. Nothing, nothing, nothing." It is unbearable.

At another flashback, later in the film, we see Nazerman arrive at the camp, where the men and women are separated. He is anxious and distraught about where they are taking his wife, and keeps looking back; the SS guard accommodates him by pulling him out of line, leading him to a barracks, plunging his head through the glass to witness the sexual degradation of the one who was half of his life. With it, Nazerman himself is utterly degraded and reduced to half a person: all he can do is dumbly watch.

The bounty of meaning in which he had once been immersed has completely vanished. There are no more extensions of his identity—everything is gone. The only thing that is unmistakably left is his physical organism, which has its own laws, and which somehow seeks to be kept alive. So Nazerman, the ex-professor, is now the Pawnbroker, keeping alive a few other refugees in New York, in a drab atmosphere of loss and constant recrimination. One of them is his mistress, but the sporadic affair is so joyless. Flesh follows out the dumb laws of its own perpetuation: food must be ingested when hungry;

fornication ensues when two members of opposite sexes crawl wearily between the same bed sheets. The organisms continue their motions, Nazerman earns the bread; but the food for the psyche, the immersion in meaning, is all dead. Nazerman's niece wants to take a vacation in Europe, and urges him to take them; but Nazerman shrugs, why go back to Europe?—it is a graveyard. And Nazerman himself is a walking corpse.

From a point of view of elemental psychology, this is perhaps the first lesson of the story: that when a man is so utterly stripped of life meaning as was Nazerman, he has no furnishings for his inner life, he is as good as dead, even though his organism gropes blindly toward life. Man is a psychic creature as well as an organismic one: tear out the meaning that sustains, and you tear literally his insides out. The remnant is a shell, as Nazerman is a tight and dry shell. Perhaps his only real error is to have survived, when everything that gave his life meaning and sustenance, died. Organisms live by bread; but man lives by meaning.

If this suggestion seems harsh, it is confirmed as the story unfolds. Being "already dead" Nazerman has to arm himself against the living, against life; and as we see him in his daily round in the pawnshop, it soon is obvious that this is exactly what he does. He has shut himself off from everyone; he is a silent automaton who pawns. There is a warm and distinguished-looking old Negro who comes to ask Nazerman an occasional question about history and philosophy; he is evidently a dilettante, self-taught, amateurish, but very bright, unassuming, and sincere. Evidently it is known to a few that

Nazerman was once a professor, but Nazerman has no intention of reviving that identity; he grudgingly tolerates the tentatives that George Smith makes to establish some kind of communication; if Nazerman is in the mood, he offers an observation or two, until he quickly loses patience and bluntly and humiliatingly ends the intercourse. He gives communication like a grudging dole.

There is also a lonely woman, not unattractive, who offers Nazerman her friendship and the possibility of love. Nazerman turns on her brutally, demands that he be left alone, insists that he has nothing in common with her, and absolutely no interest in any relationship with her. True, she is somewhat pathetic, as all isolated and lonely people are who must reach out to others in order to sustain themselves. Nazerman seems strong to these people, precisely because he is self-contained and self-sufficient; so they suffer without complaint the humiliating rebuffs at his hands, as we would suffer the scorn of a superior, believing that his anger was always due to our blunder, our presumption.

Nazerman with the impenetrable exterior; Nazerman the self-contained; Nazerman the infallible pawnbroker, who justly estimates the value of each item, and drives the proper hard bargain; Nazerman the capable, who earns a good salary in business; Nazerman the ex-professor, who so thoroughly adapts to a new life. Nazerman, what is the "secret" of your "strength"? The question is pondered by a young (Puerto-Rican?) boy who helps out in the shop. The boy wants to learn the ways of business so that he can be a success on his own.

He reasons that this is the best way to succeed, rather than going out for the fast buck, the quick and clever strike. Watch Nazerman, and learn from him. As with George Smith, the philosophical Negro, so with Jesus Ortiz, his boy-helper: Nazerman gives only the tiniest bit of himself. He consents to give the boy a few lessons in pawnbroking, partly because he evidently cannot avoid it—the boy is after all his helper. Partly too, he despises naïveness, and there is a perverse pleasure in revealing the shocking truth, in puncturing illusions. He tries to goad Ortiz about the belief in God, and then, in a rare spurt of generous revelation of his real thoughts, he discloses the ultimate measure of value: Money. "Next to the speed of light, which Einstein tells us is the only absolute in the universe, second only to that I would rank money. There, I have taught you the Pawnbroker's Credo, Ortiz. What else is there to know!"

So that was the secret, Mr. Nazerman, the Good and the True that the boy had been so patiently longing to know. The outburst of rare advice was not lost on Ortiz. This was the Einsteinian wisdom that was at the heart of life, the possession of the few learned men who really "know." Now Ortiz had no reason for hanging back for the long hard pull; he was transformed into a willful instrument who could decisively turn aside the restraining hand of his mother. Now he could make contact with the "real" models who would help him succeed in the business world: the toughs who wanted to rob the pawnshop. For a split of the take, Ortiz would now set up a robbery from the inside.

And so we see Nazerman in the typical gamut of his interhuman relationships, which reveals the second point of basic psychology contained in the story. What exactly *was* Nazerman's "secret," the source of his apparent strength? The answer can best be phrased by using those wonderfully apt words made famous by Wilhelm Reich, and by a half-century of psycho-analytic thought: "character armor." Character armor, as we know, refers literally to the arming of the personality so that it can maneuver in a threatening world. It refers to the shoring-up or damming-up of the individual's fragile sense of self-value, in order to keep that self-value safe from undermining by events and persons. In other words, character armor really refers to the whole life style that a person assumes, in order to live and act with a certain security. We all have some, because we all need to organize our personality. This organization is a process whereby some things have to be valued more than others, some acts have to be permitted, others forbidden, some lines of conduct have to be closed, some kinds of thought can be entertained, others are taboo—and so on. Each person liter-ally closes off his world, fences himself around, *in the very process of his own growth and organization.* In order to have some kind of centered control over his acts, the individual sets limits on his range of action, on the spectrum of his thought and feeling: it must all somehow be marshaled and harbored within his aegis. And this centered control is what we call the "ego": as Freud so unmistakably taught us, the ego grows partly by controlling, but also partly by constraining itself, partly by limiting its freedom of perception and action. Otherwise it would be swamped from the start.

And this limitation of perception and action is what we mean by character armor. Some people, of course, have more than others—more self-protecting constraint. This makes them remarkably stiff, as Reich saw: as though they actually wore armor. It makes them remarkably unsympathetic to points of view they have decided are not worth entertaining, or are too threatening to entertain. It shuts them very tightly toward others, who risk invading their world, and perhaps upsetting it, even if they upset it by kindness and love. Love draws one out, breaks down barriers, places the human relationship on more mutual terms: in a word, takes it somewhat *out of the control* of the armored person. It takes strength to love, simply because it takes strength to stand exposed without armor, open to the needs of others. In characterological terms, the ability to stand open to love is a sort of heroism.

So we can understand Nazerman's "secret," the source of his apparent strength. We can understand, too, that his strength was truly apparent, not real. And the secret is that he had no secret, but was really a pathetically fragile soul, trying to keep thoughts, things, and persons from destroying his gravely wounded psyche. Nazerman the ravaged; Nazerman the weak; Nazerman with threatening memories unbearable in their painfulness; Nazerman the refugee, still in the world of the living by chance; Nazerman with a flickering sense of warmth about himself; Nazerman the cold and damp, the dreary; Nazerman the ghost buffeted about by the chill air of a dead and horrible past. Above all, Nazerman the empty, Nazerman whose soul was without furnishings, whose life and world were without meaning.

If we understand this well, it brings us to another and related aspect of basic psychology—the universal problem of "fetishization." Fetishization means the organization of perception and action, by the personality, around a very striking and compelling—but narrow—theme. It follows from what we have said, that if everybody has some character armor, everyone is also somewhat of a fetishist. If you are obliged to close yourself to the multiplicity of things, it follows that you will focus somewhat on a restrained area of things; and, if you cannot freely value everything, nor freely weigh all things against all other things, then, you must give disproportionate weight to some things *which do not deserve* this weight. You artificially inflate a small area of the world, give it a higher value in the horizon of your perception and action. And you do this because it represents an area that you can *firmly hold on to,* that you can *skillfully manipulate,* that you can *use easily to justify yourself*—your actions, your sense of self, your option in the world. The fetish, in a word, is an arbitrary focus for your derivation of self-value.

It follows that people who are more secure in their sense of self, more daring in their action, more open in their armor, will tend to fetishize less. And conversely, that people who are more dammed-up, weaker, more constricted in what they can safely undertake and think, will fetishize more. It follows, too, from our story, that Nazerman, having lost the plenitude of meaning of his past life and identity, had to refocus his personality around a more narrow and striking source of meaning, of self-sustenance. He could marshal so little of personal resources, so shallow a spectrum of meaning, that he had to grasp on to some firm and easy source in order to pull his world together. After the defeat of his psyche in the loss of his loved objects and entire past life, he would disintegrate completely unless he found some ready substitute. And this new fetish was the god Money. Just as in the ancient world the invention of coinage had saved the psyche of the Mediterranean peoples, who were thrown out of the integral and meaningful communitarian life under God and Nature, so in the modern world the fetish of money continues to fulfill this time-worn and vital task. As Marx and Simmel taught us, money is focused power, a point of orientation for the whole self-feeling of the personality, a locus around which one can justify an entire way of life. It is true power because it liberates us from the constraints of family, community, and friendship: with it we can go anywhere, do anything. And it is false power because it cuts off several dimensions of our lives and puts only one in their place: it cuts off community and the appeal of man; it cuts off God and self-transcending duty; and it replaces them with the narrow infallibility of material calculation. It is true power because one's vital sense of self is no longer immersed in a network of obligations, some of which are truly constricting and even negating. It is false power because it encapsulates one's sense of self in a chest of gold coins, or in a bank book with numbered pages. In a word, the fetish of money is a real organizing point for the personality—as all striking fetishes are; and at the same time, it is a false god, because it throws us back on ourselves and cuts off the richness of the world.

So Nazerman: a tattered psyche padded with sheafs of silver certificates. If we now understand what made Nazerman "tick" in terms of basic psychological theory, we are ready to continue our story after this digression. Because only now are we in a position to understand the rest, Nazerman's inevitable decline and final defeat. If indeed he was weak and not strong, fetishized and not broad, then he will be unable to stand in the face of the buffetings to which he is subject in the story. And this is another lesson of basic psychology: namely, that the person who is armored, and who is fetishized, will be able to maneuver well only so long as his world is not too threatened. If he has been able to organize his personality around narrow themes, and adapt to his world, this is partly accomplished by giving up the one really great strength that man needs in a crisis: I mean the ability to adapt to continually new kinds of stimuli, the ability to change, and grow, shed old armor, and broaden away from fetishes.

In our story Nazerman was subjected to two great buffetings by events. The first was implacable, really too much from the start: the terrible memories of his past which haunted him. The whole episode of the Nazi terror, as revealed in a few flashbacks, is important not for what it represented in itself, but for what it did to Nazerman. The film was not a story about what happened in Germany, but the story of Nazerman in New York. And he simply could not keep these memories out, they kept obtruding into his life, upsetting it, rendering it valueless and *meaningless* by contrast. It gradually becomes plain in the story that the only real sliver of meaning that Nazerman has is his own survival as an organism, and the upkeep of a few other refugees. But this does not sustain him against the memories—they keep breaking through the walls of his ego. After all, he is weak. When this happens, it also dilutes his character armor. Unable to close his ego off against the past from within, it is of no avail to close his person off to people and events around him. And as he is gradually undermined from within, his hard exterior also crumbles. It is like a flood against a wall of sand. This is conveyed beautifully in the sequence in the film that to many seemed extraneous: I mean when he searches out the woman who had offered him friendship and love and whom he had so brutally rejected. Now he talks to her, tells her a bit about himself, about how he has these memories from the past which trouble him more and more. It is obvious that he is opening himself up because he is being undermined from within, and not because his character is naturally mellowing. The woman interprets his cry for help as a new warmth and friendship, but she is quickly disillusioned as is the spectator: the Pawnbroker is not acting from a position of strength, but from one of desperation. His armor is opened, but against his will; he is in no shape to sustain the mutuality of a friendship, and he quickly shrugs off her proffered hand, and stumbles out of her apartment. His apparent relaxation and interpersonal mellowness was merely an inner groan which had to be communicated—but no one could be an island of refuge to a man caught in Nazerman's flood.

The other great buffeting to which he was subject is allied naturally to the first. It proved to be the breaking point for his character. This was when he found out that the money he was being paid to run the pawnshop came from the earnings of prostitutes. The pawnshop is after all only a "front" for other operations, and Nazerman earns his large salary by serving as a respectable front man. He knows this, but what increasingly troubles him is that Murillio's "other" operations might also include the brothel down the street. There is the frightening scene when his racketeering Negro employer, Murillio, confirms this to Nazerman, and Nazerman is stunned, overwhelmed. The employer has his own thick armor, and has dammed himself up against the world by excluding any sensitivity to suffering. He is a bit surprised that Nazerman, whom he had given credit for worldly wisdom and strength, is so upset about the source of his salary. And we might be surprised too, if we did not know that money was Nazerman's last remaining fetish: the sole source of his self-esteem. In a word, this last source *had to remain pure and unsullied,* had to be irreproachable, or its value as a focus for organizing Nazerman's sense of self was vitally attacked. And this is just what happened. No longer was Nazerman the independent and irreproachable provider, who made possible a new life in the New World for a few refugee souls, a life without pretense and sham, a life frankly based on money, honestly earned and generously dispensed. No longer was Nazerman wise in his disillusionment, clever in his readaptation, clean in the basic predicate of his life. No! He was none of these things; if anything, he was the opposite: stupid, because he still lived on illusions; dirty, because *his life was still made possible by the degrading sacrifice of other lives.* After all, his life was borrowed from the dead: his survival was literally on the corpses of his family; he escaped to the New World from the graveyard of Europe; he lived a borrowed mandate, borrowed from the sacrifice of his loved ones. And now this terrible vicariousness was *continuing:* he lived on prostitutes' earnings.

Of course Murillio could not understand Nazerman's total collapse in the face of this revelation. He thought that it was merely the moralistic finickiness of a basically bourgeois spirit. So he could show nothing but contempt for Nazerman's apparent scruples. He didn't realize what it meant for Nazerman to have his fetish destroyed by the undermining of its unambiguous purity: it meant literally that the New World too, had become a graveyard for Nazerman. So Nazerman might even have consented to die on the spot, to melt into the graveyard. But his employer was not obliging: one had to pay for one's illusions by continuing to live. He didn't realize the kind of sentence this meant for the Pawnbroker in psychological terms: it meant continuing to live and act without armor, without a centering ego. Nazerman proceeded to disintegrate at work: the fetish of money, dissolved, he no longer could organize his thoughts, and he offered huge prices for worthless items, and ridiculously small prices for choice items. His boy-helper saw that something terrible was wrong with Nazerman, who had suddenly lost his business sense and seemed sick.

But it was too late, both for Nazerman and for the boy. For it is just at this time that the holdup the boy had set up and facilitated was to take place. As the film nears its end, the tragic becomes absurd: here are the young toughs waving a gun in Nazerman's face—Nazerman who is already psychically dead, and wants nothing better than to put physical closure on his death. Instead of opening the safe and giving them the money, he sees his chance for death, and pushes the safe door shut. One of the youths, in desperation and threat, aims a shot at Nazerman, but the boy-helper screams out not to harm the old man, and lunges into the path of the bullet. It strikes him instead of Nazerman. He staggers out to the sidewalk and collapses in the spurting of his own life blood.

Nazerman the half-dead reels out of the pawnshop and falls kneeling over the boy as the street crowd begins to mill around. With an animal sound and an expression of anguish for which Steiger has no equal, Nazerman looks up to the faces and to the sky. What was the terrible existential shock that now convulsed the wreck of his being? It could be nothing else than the adumbration that once again, and finally, his life was made possible by the death of others. Even in wanting to die, he had inadvertently caused the death of the boy, contributed to the stifling of another life. And if he could have reasoned at this moment—which, of course, he could not—he would also have been able to understand that truly he had caused the death of the boy, in a much more direct way: he had given him the very advice, to live for the god Money, that led the boy to stage the holdup in the first place. In other words, by the needs of his own character armor, he had evangelized for a false god, converted an innocent soul to a sullied fetish. In this deeper way, the condition for his own survival helped destroy another life: he was entirely guilty. Nazerman the complete ghoul on the living.

We can imagine the state of Nazerman at this moment: onrushing images from the past with their excruciating painfulness; the complete dissolution of character armor by which to organize and shut out the present; the grotesque *dénouement of* his own desire for death—instead, the death of the innocent boy. Nazerman is overwhelmed by the world, it swirls around and inside him. All *meaning* is gone, the whole thing is senseless, there are no proper relationships, no commensurate connections, it is absurd and disgusting. Nazerman swirls with the rush of images and sensations, he has no firm center, he is being carried away. And here is where the screen version departs radically from Wallant's story, and yet gives an integral portrait that is astonishingly apt in terms of basic psychology. Nazerman staggers back into the pawnshop, or better, *is* staggered back into the pawnshop: for at this moment he has only one thing left, the thing he carried away from Europe—his organism, with hardly an ego to propel it. It is now the only point of orientation left, the only focus for some kind of meaningful sensation, the only locus for some kind of control, the only thing that can be pinned down in the whirl of absurdity. And pin it down he does, literally, as he leans down on the paper spindle on the counter, with one hand placed over the other, and gradually works the spindle through the palms of his hands.

The pain must be excruciating, but oh! what a relief: for one brief interval the whirl stops, the empty organism becomes a center, a full, pulsating and painful center, with some kind of control over the flux of sensation, even if that control is earned by self-mutilation and self-sacrifice. It is the last point at which some kind of purposeful action can be initiated, the last island where a meaningful sequence can be pieced together: "I place my hands, I press, I feel pain to my brain and bowels, something exists in a spectrum of steady time and under my aegis." This is the same kind of desperate saving action that we observe in the self-mutilations of schizophrenics, and in primitives who try to stimulate rainfall by opening their veins and splashing blood on a rock. It is a ritual creation of meaning from a position of almost complete inferiority and helplessness. But Nazerman is now kin to the schizophrenic, not the primitive: he is wholly disorganized and defeated, there is nothing to sustain him, no pattern of meaning into which to fit his act. He staggers out of the pawnshop and leans, head buried and hands upraised and bleeding, against a wall. There is nothing more we can learn from his sufferings, and the film fades out.

But the story leaves one thing for us to ponder, and it may be the most important of all, the final thrust of insight that crowns the whole work, draws the circle on it, gives it its deeper sense. I mean, of course, the relationship between Nazerman's pierced hands and the stigmata of Christ, and the similarity of their names: Nazerman, Nazarene. The end of *The Pawnbroker* reveals the Christ theme: when the universe is overwhelming with the senselessness of suffering, when the whole world cries for an explanation which no man of flesh can give, what is one to do? The thing that tortured Nazerman was that he was absolutely powerless to *do* anything in the face of suffering: he could only helplessly surrender his children and his wife; he could only consent to eat the bread earned on prostitution; he could only be forced to witness the gratuitous murder of an innocent youth. He had the terrible twofold burden of man, a burden that has weighed him down since self-conscious life emerged over a million years ago: to *witness* suffering without being able to overcome it; and to *bear the guilt* of causing suffering, by the fact that one's life has unintended yet unavoidable repercussions on others, simply because one *takes up space and moves about as an organism*. This is what religious mythology so beautifully points to as the "fall into sin of created life."

The only way to heal this rupture of the fall is to follow it in the only direction it leads: to humble oneself completely, to allow oneself to be destroyed, to take the burden of guilt and powerlessness, and to sanctify them in the sacrifice of oneself. Thereby one links his existence back into a higher ground of meaning: one suffers because it is God's purpose for creation; man is the tool for purposes he cannot understand, but which transcend him and his well-being. The promise is that this very defeat can be turned into victory, ultimately, because if man can do nothing, the Creator can do all things in His own good time. This is the promise of Redemption, that somehow God will make good man's absurd fate, man's living sacrifice. That is why the sacrifice must ideally be made in joy; sadness is a sin in Judeo-Christian thought because it reflects a lack of faith in God's design. The meaninglessness of life is only apparent; innocent death is the ultimate fulfillment of Divine purpose. We see this idea already adumbrated in Oedipus at Colonus:

Oedipus who protests his innocence, knows that his suffering
is unmerited and that precisely thereby is he sanctified, and
claims that where he will be buried the land will be fulfilled.
And before Sophocles, variations of the idea were familiar to
primitive tribes: the ritual of the innocent scapegoat who carries
off the guilt and sin of the tribe, and becomes thereby a healing
instrument for all its members. From earliest times man had to
reforge the link between his pitiful finitude and the deeper
purposes of Creation. This was the peculiarly human burden,
the burden of a self-conscious animal. With the advent of
Judeo-Christianity, the healing symbol became the common
property of Western man. In the figure of Christ we have the
innocent scapegoat who dies for the sins of all mankind, not
only the tribe; the Son of God who proves that since even
God's flesh must be humiliated on earth, there is no escape from
it for lesser men; the scapegoat who is resurrected, and so
proves that living sacrifice is not in vain.

When we consider the symbol in its purity and its historical
meaning we can see where the similarity of Nazerman to the
Nazarene ends. There is a difference between the disintegration
of a shallow and fetishized personality, and the sacrifice of a
saint. The yielding up of innocent life is similar, but not the
quality of the lives they lived. In death every man becomes the
instrument of God, but in life each serves differently. Nazerman served in the worst possible way, by all religious ideals:
every life he touched he caused to shrink back upon itself because he himself was so closed off and afraid. The saint lives
openly, with an absolute minimum of character armor, and so

each life that he touches is enriched by his sympathy, generosity, and true fearlessness. How can one live openly unless he is fearless, since we put on character armor because of our fears? And how can one be fearless unless he is willing to let go of life, to make the very meaning of his life the sacrifice of it? This was the real "secret" of Christ's strength, a "secret" that Nazerman did not know. Nazerman's life was centered wholly on himself, on the need for survival; this was the direction of meaning that he followed after the horrors of Europe. He organized his personality around the fetish of money, and it was this false god that did him in. Money is not ultimate, not above the world, but contingent upon it, contaminated by it, as Nazerman was to learn. By choosing this source of strength, instead of God, Nazerman cut off the only dimension in which he could grow and mellow, the only one that would make ultimate sense out of his continued struggles.

This is the paradox and the final lesson of basic psychology that our story contains. We see with complete clarity why people lead "repressed" lives, why they arm themselves against the world, why they close their personhood down to a narrow focus of control and meaning: the academicians, the military, the workingmen, the administrators—all men, in fact, except the religious genius. To open oneself completely means that one invites the world to invade oneself, it means to weaken one's center, to expose oneself to the threat of absolute meaninglessness. Furthermore, it invites the scoffing and denigration by one's fellow men. People snigger at the open person, shrug their shoulders at him, distrust him, hound him and snap at him, just as Nazerman did to those who crossed his life in the pawnshop. And how can it be otherwise—isn't the open person a threat to the closed one? Doesn't he oblige the open one to let his guard down, to relax and mellow a bit, to practice tentativeness, to see the world in shades of gray instead of harsh contrasts, to exercise sympathy, perhaps even love? All these things the weak person cannot do, which is why he armored himself in the first place. Besides, the open person gives no appearance of strength, he seems pathetic in his naïve trust, his childlike confidence. His tentativeness seems like hesitation, his soft approach seems like timid appeasement. As he reveals his inmost thoughts, he exposes his "insides," and there is soon nothing left for us to be interested in. He seems shallow, dispossessed of "secrets," of murky depths that fascinate, of subterranean walls that hold back deep and rumbling passions and unknown reserves of strength. All these things the closed person gives the appearance of, and so we respect him, handle him gently, fear him. How can one think of changing one identity for the other, in the predatory world of men? To become open means to become a complete masochist.

And this is the genius of the religious genius: that he becomes a masochist to the world from a position of strength and by choice. He disperses the center of his personality by shedding his character armor, but this is only an apparent dispersal, not a real one: it is only a dispersal of one's center *in the world*. His secret is that he re-centers himself beyond the world, by making the meaning of life dependent on the ultimate source of meaning, not on the worldly one. So he has nothing to lose in the world, because he has nothing to gain in it. He knows that basically he can do nothing here, expect nothing here; so he can become completely humble, passive, as nothing. This is a passivity that achieves its fulfillment in destruction, which is why so few can understand it, sanction it, or want to imitate it. Nietzsche was appalled by this ideal of the "Christian slave" and vented his whole fury on it: he understood that it undermines man's peculiar task on this planet—to make something out of it. In the world's terms the religious genius is "crazy," and perhaps rightly so, since it is more than can be asked of the mass of men: they must live and work and continue on.

Whatever side our personal sentiments may be on, we can see that the problem is no simple one: the ideal of the open self versus the pragmatism of the armored self is a dialectic that points beyond psychology to the questions of evolution and human destiny. Any dialogue that really has meaning for man must begin here. It is clear that psychology can only serve its purpose if it leads us to this point, gives us a just understanding of the conditions of human action *only so that we can begin* to ponder intelligently the wider questions of man's fate. *The Pawnbroker* is a true work of art precisely because it points beyond what it reveals.

AUGUST, 1967

Notes

1. As we will see, in the film version it is Nazerman himself who is the innocent sacrifice, the Christ figure. In the story, Wallant evidently intended Jesus Ortiz, the boy-helper in the pawnshop, to symbolize this sacrifice, while Nazerman himself remains alive in order to continue the ancient role of the Jew—to mourn in the world where God is absent.

IV | BUÑUEL AND THE DEMONIC

The last revelation of intellect and sentiment is that in a manner it severs the man from all other men; makes known to him that the spiritual powers are sufficient to him if no other being existed; that he is to deal absolutely in the world, as if he alone were a system and a state, and though all should perish could make all anew.

EMERSON

THERE ARE a few persons in each epoch with whom one must come to grips, simply because they are the ones who are struggling with the deeper meaning of the epoch; and if we want to know that meaning we have to unravel their struggles. With the intellectual spokesman, this process is easy, since he is explicit. With the artist, it may be extremely difficult, since his message is in an emotional form, it is non-discursive. Luis Buñuel, the noted film director, is one such emotional spokesman for our time; and many have been at some pains to decipher just what he is trying to say.

From his early films in Spain, he showed himself to be an uncompromising realist; from later works such as *Viridiana,* a shocking sadist. His films undermine "public morality"—which is why he was twice banished from his native country. This official judgment happens to be the most apt one: whatever else Buñuel may be in the art of film-making, he is first and foremost a moralist. And what is the moralist if not a consummate realist, and largely a sadist—as the Marquis de Sade taught us? He is out to undermine public morality precisely because he is propagandizing for kinds of individual freedom that a hypocritical public morality does not allow. In this sense Buñuel is a modern Sade; but the comparison ends there: Buñuel is a larger man, with a keener social psychology, and a healthier social conscience.

The document for my remarks is his film *The Exterminating Angel*. Here surely is the consummate moral allegory for our time, directly in the tradition of Rousseau, Emerson, and Nietzsche. As a work of art, its merits can certainly be debated, and I'm not exactly fitted for this kind of debate; but its moralistic teaching is beyond question, and this is what I want briefly to explore.

The entire story takes place in a large private home, in Mexico. The protagonists are wealthy, socialite types: artists, professionals. The host is giving a dinner party for some friends. It is all quite a routine affair. In fact, it is so routine that the host hopes to highlight it with a few surprises, and he seems to have bought a sheep and a bear to use in some unexpected manner during the evening. We are given to understand that these kinds of tricks are themselves quite routine for this host; but right from the beginning of the film we are also given to understand that something is quite different about this dinner party—quite ominous in fact. We see it in the behavior of the staff of servants: none of them, with the exception of the head butler, wants to remain in the house. Each contrives some kind of excuse to leave after the meal has been prepared and as soon as the guests begin arriving. Even the threats of the master of the house and of the butler, to dismiss them permanently from their posts if they leave, are of no avail. They each leave the house in anxious haste, as if a plague were about to descend upon it. It is all very strange.

Yet the dinner takes place without any unusual event. These are stuffy types, bourgeois in their habits, bourgeois even in their attacks on morality—as when they chide the virgin among them for her chastity. They are pampered, stiff, each one alone in his narrow little world with its uninteresting cares. In a word, a typical human group, a cross-section of *Homo sapiens* in our time, from among the privileged strata of society. Yes, above all, they are properly social. We see this proper sociality as the evening wears on. One of them is enjoined to play a piece on the piano, and then an encore, but she refuses, she is tired. Someone wants to make a move to leave, but no one else seems to be leaving, so he doesn't dare make the simple move. What does this host have on his mind anyway? The evening is wearing on, it is rather boring; good form would have the party end—is the host's "joke" in the fact that he intends them all to spend the night, right there? He really is a card. It is hardly amusing, and yet, what to do? Someone removes his dinner jacket, almost a capital sin in countries south of the border; the host finds it revolting; egotistic self-indulgence. People begin flopping down on the sofa and drowsing off.

Perhaps some refreshments would be in order, one has only to step out of the room to get them.

But now, something strange. In this most usual of evenings, in this most typical of upper-class homes, with this most pedestrian elite gathering, something truly unexpected and uncanny has occurred: by some mysterious power, which seems to have descended on the group, *no one can leave the room*, no one can move beyond the edge of the room into the adjoining one. Try as they will, they cannot move beyond the border. They are helplessly trapped in one room by some ineluctable, invisible force.

Here Buñuel's story follows the model of Kafka: at a given point, in order to bring home his message with maximum force, he steps off the brink from matter-of-fact realism into a truly fantastic realism. The rest of the film is such an excursion. The group in the room becomes increasingly elemental; the social niceties which sustained them are gradually given up. It is a survival situation. Bodily functions are performed in one of the closets. One couple moves into a closet in order to fornicate—it is "the end" so what the hell. Others suffer hallucinations. After a day or so, the problem of thirst becomes unbearable until someone thinks of hacking into the wall and exposing the water pipe. Hunger begins to gnaw until the sheep, which was to serve in some way as a surprise for the party, walks down the stairs of the next room and goes into their room. They would tear the animal to pieces, but quickly skin it and roast it on a fire built on the floor. The bear also descends the stairs, but ignores the room and goes on out of the house. Outside, a cordon of police and friends, who try to move toward the house but are prevented by some invisible force from approaching very near. Even a child who tries cannot penetrate the barrier.

But what is this trip into the fantastic, what does it mean? Several of the people in the group believe that the blocked exit is a trick of the host, a trick that somehow got out of hand, or a trick stemming from his deep malevolence toward them. Thus the ordeal takes a turn into an elemental paranoia, and near the end of it several of the group demand the host's blood as a retribution for their sufferings. The host, gentleman to the end, consents to take his own life to show the purity of his conscience, and also perhaps to make some kind of desperate, remedial gesture that might lift the curse they are under.

And it is just at this point that the virgin notices something, as if in a revelation: that the positions of the people in the room are very close to what they were at a certain point in the party, on the very first night. It was the point at which the piano performer had just declined to give an encore. The virgin asks them all to take exactly the same places they had then, and to repeat the exact conversation leading up to that moment; and then she asks the person who was talking to the piano performer to say what was on his mind, instead of the words he actually uttered. He reveals that he wanted to bid everyone goodnight and leave the party. In a hush of anxious expectation the virgin asks him to utter just that thought and to move to leave the room. He does so, and everyone else starts to follow —and lo! the spell is lifted, and the degraded, filthy, and haggard band stumble hysterically out of the room and on outside to freedom.

The very next scene takes place in the local church, as the same group, now recovered and cleaned up, very much their former selves, is assembled to give thanks for their liberation. As the priest makes the routine motions of benediction and utters the routine Latin words, the group kneels in routine obedience. In a few moments the absurd abruptly descends once again on these innocent victims; they find that they cannot get out of the church. The scene shifts to the outside at the very same moment as a flock of sheep runs rapidly through the square and into the church. Off to the other side of the square, a whole milling throng of people tries to advance on the church—it is not clear why; but what is clear is that a cordon of police with clubs beats them back as the film fades out.

The ending, of course, is a short symbolic repetition of the main theme, with an added twist. And it becomes obvious to many, from this striking repetition, what Buñuel intended. Large student audiences, to whom I assigned a viewing of the film, suddenly experience the gnawing anxiety that the exits to the movie hall may be impenetrable. Whether they understand explicitly what Buñuel is driving at, they experience emotionally his message, from the hour and a half of helpless passivity in which they underwent the buffetings of his slashing realism. Buñuel is telling them nothing more complicated than the fact that a veritable curse descends on man when he acts the role of the passive spectator sheep rather than of the willful executor free subject. The decisive point of the film, that carried this message, was of course the moment when the guest who *wanted* to leave the party did *not dare express* his *spontaneous, organismic, energetic desire* for *fear* of violating the *social conventional forms* of action. Only when this fault was remedied, by re-enacting the sequence and moving willfully out of the room, could the curse be lifted, the curse of the Exterminating Angel.

When we understand this basic message and the crucial point of the film, we get a rough idea of Buñuel's symbolism: the sheep, of course, went to join its kin in the room and, later, in the church; the bear, symbol of more virile life forces, passed the room by, ignored it. The servants, who sensed something wrong with the evening, may also have symbolized a more earthy and less affected proletariat. Perhaps Buñuel intended the virgin to symbolize life force in its uncorruptedness—she was the only complex, self-reliant character—and so it was given to her to intuit what went wrong, and provide the key to freeing the group. Even childlike innocence was not strong enough to break the spell. The whole fantastic episode of the group's imprisonment in the room was, as we said, a Kafka-like technique, designed to highlight the major message, to show the exaggerated troubles that followed a simple sequence of erroneous acts. It was a commentary on the main message, and not itself the meaning of the film. Perhaps it overloaded the film as a few have suggested: the long sequence of the sufferings of the group, following upon the simple failure of one of them to express his spontaneous desire, may be artistically out of balance. Perhaps the symbolism also is too transparent. But if Buñuel showed his usually heavy hand as a film director, he cannot be accused of being philosophically superficial or clumsy. In fact, the film taken as a whole is nothing less than an artistic rendering of the great philosophical-ontological theme of our time: the conditions of the defeat of human life, the activating of The Exterminating Angel, or The Demonic. And this is what I want briefly to dwell upon.

Of all writers on The Demonic, I know of no one who has given a richer treatment, from an ontological point of view, than Paul Tillich in his famous essay by that title,[1] and in scattered passages in his other writings. Romano Guardini also has some excellent things to say.[2] There is no point in my repeating poorly what Tillich especially has already said with such incomparable mastery, or in trying to discuss The Demonic in more than one of its dimensions. All I want to do is show how well Buñuel has artistically conveyed one of the major dimensions of The Demonic for man in our time. In fact, it is *the* major one. First of all, let us be clear about what we mean by The Demonic. When man talks about the eruption of evil into the human realm, he is not pretending to describe what is working in the background forces of nature; he cannot know this. But what he can know is what is peculiarly defeating human life, as this defeat manifests itself in the realm of human action. To talk about The Demonic, then, as the peculiar manifestation of evil in the affairs of men, is to talk about something that can be described, seen, and understood. It is a way of coming to grips with the defeat of life on the surface of life, and not in the bowels of nature. I say this to quiet those modern philosophers who object to all loose talk, and who remind us that after Kant and Sir William Hamilton no one can pretend to know what is working behind things.

In the realm of human affairs The Demonic is real. It is engendered by the acts of men, or better, to use Buñuel's allegory, by the *failure* of men to act. Specifically, it comes into being when men fail to act *individually* and *willfully,* on the basis of their own *personal, responsible* powers. The Demonic refers specifically to the creation of power by groups of men who blindly follow authority and convention, power which then engulfs them and defeats them. Let us also note that The Demonic has a naturalistic basis. It comes into being on the basis of a real evolutionary development: man is the animal in nature who, par excellence, can create vast structures of power by means of his symbolic manipulation of the world of energy. He can create far vaster structures of power than those other highly organized and powerful group animals, the Hymenoptera. But here is where a certain irony of evolution enters the picture. Man creates a much higher potential of power than the ants or bees, but he does it in much the same way that these insects do: that is, by giving his allegiance to groups, since power can only be created maximally by large numbers of individuals working together in institutions; and by giving his allegiance to leaders who manipulate and direct the use of that power. The irony is that in the realm of aspiringly free creatures, structures of power become enslaving over the very individuals who contribute to their creation: the group dominates the individual, and the leaders manipulate the groups.

So we can see that evolution has presented a veritable paradox in the emergence of man: here is an animal whose means of creating power are such that they check his own free development. But man is not a Hymenoptera. The way out of the paradox is that man is the one animal created by evolution who can use his power for the further liberation of *individuals,* from the continuing constraint of groups. This liberation would theoretically come about as the disposition over power is made a matter of increasingly responsible individual decision. Instead of blindly following the leader and creating power for a world that he cannot control and has no say in, man would at all times question the leadership and disposition of power, the ends for which it is used. In this way he would not offer limitless power to isolated individuals who lead men, or to the automatic functioning of institutions into which men submissively fit; rather, he would spread power for the fullest liberation of the subjectivities of masses of individuals, would continually review the ends of the institutions that dispose of power, and make these institutions responsible to new human motives, new human needs. In a word, he would use his unique capacity to symbolize, to control the power unleashed uniquely by that capacity. The paradox of evolution would be overcome.

Put this way, we need no reminding that this is the authentic and basic meaning of the promise of democracy: that it would be the one form of government most in accord with the promise of evolution itself, and that it would seek to turn the paradox of evolution to the fullest development of man's subjectivity. Democracy is the form of government that has taken upon itself the task of combating The Demonic, by making each person all find in himself and a responsible, self-reliant point of authority to which power leaders and power institutions are beholden. If the promise of democracy cannot be realized, then evolution itself will be defeated in its highest creation, and The Demonic will enslave man and then destroy him. Yet we see just this happening in our time, which is why Buñuel's allegory is so apt to the present social crisis. Power has become free-floating, precisely because there are no self-reliant men; instead, there are masses led by demagogues, masses who create the power that the demagogues use, and who pass on the decisions over that power to those demagogues. (See Figure A for a crude illustration.) "The Great Leader knows best. Let the experts decide, they have the intimate knowledge. We cannot make the decisions in areas outside our competence." From what we have said, it is obvious that these are not merely the words of slavish and helpless masses: they are the death groan of evolution itself. The fact is that the Great Leaders may not know best. They have made empires crumble and caused untold sufferings among their own peoples since biblical times, as history attests. The fact is that experts cannot decide since they see only a small segment of the whole picture, and cannot weigh the ends of action in their totality. The terrible blundering wars of modern times, fought with the weapons the experts created, are testimony enough to this. The promise of democracy knew these things, which is why it was anti-expert and anti-leader. It knew that the leader had to be controlled by responsible and willful masses of men, precisely because he will be corrupted by power into making decisions that are self-defeating. Whether he knows it or not, or admits it or not, the leader needs to be curbed, needs the broadest base of self-limiting decisions. The power created by vast institutions has to be literally anchored down into the individualities who man the institutions, otherwise it will engulf them as well as the leaders. (See Figure B for a crude illustration.)

As Tillich already saw in pre-World War II Europe, and as we are seeing today, once the vast powers of institutions become free-floating, subject only to the decisions of leaders who are themselves out of control, The Demonic takes over in full force. The structure of power descends over men, and has its way with them. The institutions literally run under their own weight, pulled ahead by the ominous overhanging cloud of power. Nothing that any one individual, or any small group, can do, seems to be of any avail—matters only seem to get worse. The reason is that as long as a general consensus is maintained, the main manipulators of power direct themselves to eliminating anything that hinders the smooth flow of the largest body of power. Individual and small groups of dissidents only serve to arouse the anxiety of the masses, and since the masses do not control the power, their anxiety gives an even greater mandate to the leaders to use the power without restraint. We might say that both the helplessness of the masses and their heightened anxiety in the face of social conflict give the leaders a double mandate. What seems to happen is that small pockets of power cancel themselves out—left against right, young against old, small group against small group— while the main thrust of power grows in its coerciveness. This is very much what happened in the rise of Fascism in pre-

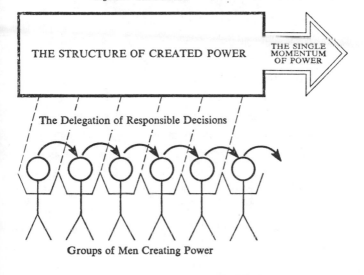

Figure A **The Demonic**

THE STRUCTURE OF CREATED POWER

THE SINGLE MOMENTUM OF POWER

The Delegation of Responsible Decisions

Groups of Men Creating Power

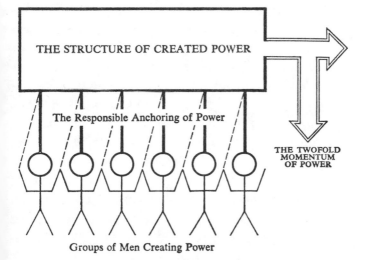

Figure B **The Democratic**

THE STRUCTURE OF CREATED POWER

THE TWOFOLD MOMENTUM OF POWER

The Responsible Anchoring of Power

Groups of Men Creating Power

World War II Europe, and what is happening in the United States today. And all this, as we said, because there is not the broadest possible base of control, an anchoring of power in as many subjectivities as there are those who fashion it—this would check and balance it, as the early theorists of democracy saw. Instead, the new structures of power churn on and jerk the huge conglomerates of modern men.

Yes, these are perhaps clever enough schema, the reader might say, and put in this crude way, The Demonic seems real enough. But how can we ever imagine that the structures of power will actually be anchored in self-reliant and responsible individuals; how can the masses of men ever achieve the development and personal quality necessary to such a task? It is all a hopeless ideal, impossible in the world of the real. We need leaders, and we need experts and we will always have the elite few to make the decisions for the masses. Society cannot function without structures, otherwise it is anarchy. Granted that structures objectify the human spirit, make of man more of a manipulated thing than a free center who controls things. How can it be otherwise? If evolution gave us the paradox of an animal who unleashes maximum power only to better enslave himself, this is a paradox we have to work within as best we can; it is not a paradox that we can hope to overcome.

So reasons the skeptical mind, the tough realist. No doubt he is right enough to be realistic and skeptical, yet his objections are hardly new. The fact is that this matter was fully thought out and argued among the social theorists of the nineteenth century, and the best they could do was pass it on to us. But they also passed on the hope and promise of democracy. I mean that if we assume the skeptical position, we are admitting that democracy itself is an unrealizable ideal, and we may as well forget it. This is the hard choice before us: accept The Demonic and negate the promise of democracy; fight The Demonic, and assume a Quixotic posture for the realization of a hopeless ideal. Many of our brightest minds are today doing just the former thing: watering down the ideal of democracy to make it accord more with a managerial elite philosophy and a fatalistic acceptance of the structure of things. The point is that in matters of ideal visions, man has a choice: he can choose to work for them or not. But as our times are teaching us, the choice is only illusory. The fact is that we cannot shirk the task of working for the impossible ideal because to do so means the utter defeat of promise of human freedom, of the further thrust of evolution through the unlimited development of individual persons. It is a matter of free subjectivity against constraining objectivity, *et voilà tout.*

This is where the ending of Buñuel's allegory is itself so strikingly apt as a summation of the main theme of our times: in the church, the passive human sheep, once again trapped by their automatic and uncritical acceptance of the way things are, of the word of the leader, of the symbols of authority and convention. They are joined by a galloping flock of fellow sheep. But now a new twist, a glimmer of something else. Outside, in the square, the masses of men seem to be rising in protest, trying to move ahead and break into The Demonic, with some kind of new adaptation, some kind of release of new energies from the bowels of nature. In between, the cordon of police, the guardians of the ossified structure of things, wielding their clubs and beating back the youthful masses of men. It is a panoramic tableau that is spreading all over the world: new and potentially free men pushing against the structure, crying for new forms of adaptations, and being beaten back by new and sophisticated forms of repression, devised and used by the very powers and leaders that the masses have created and entrenched. We see it in the Detroit ghettos, in Vietnam, in all the big urban centers of East and West, in the communist as well as in the capitalist countries. It is not a matter of ideology. Change the faces and labels of the antagonists, the struggle is the same: unknown human energies against encrusted social forms. How it will come out only history will tell. Our task is to recognize it as the pulsating ebb and flow of evolution itself, and to carefully decide where our responsible option lies. Nor is the matter hopeless. If modern man has recognized The Demonic as the problem of his own further development, this gives him some purchase for eventually triumphing over the problem. Furthermore, since Marx, he has been able to pinpoint the exact rooting of The Demonic mainly in unexamined economic structures. This is the localization of the disease of evolution, in which man has made his own diagnosis. Man's critical intellect guides the human spirit as it presses into the world. In ways that are yet unknown to us, this spirit will continue giving birth to its own possibilities.

SEPTEMBER, 1967

Notes

1. In *The Interpretation of History*, New York: Scribner's, 1936.
2. In *Power and Responsibility*, Chicago: Regnery, 1961.

V | PARANOIA

The Poetics of
the Human Condition

Indeed, the common phrase for insanity is . . . a misleading
one. The madman is not the man who has lost his reason.
The madman is the man who has lost everything except his
reason.

G. K. CHESTERTON *(1908, p. 19)*

I.

THE MORE we study man the more the striking realization dawns that what we call perversity is really an impoverished poetry, a creative ingenuity from a desperate position. And this is, after all, a definition of even the best poetry: a cry, a reaching out, an attempt to make sense, with patterns of words, of the confines of the human condition.

Nowhere is this more clear than in the behavior that we call paranoia. And here, as in many other places, psychiatry and psychoanalysis have led us astray. Paranoia is a psychiatric word, from the Greek *para* and *nous,* literally, "beside the mind." But it is just not this at all, as Chesterton so well understood: paranoia is really the most intense and focused functioning of the mind. It is mind *alone,* trying to make sense out of experience for an impoverished, weak, and frightened organism, for an organism that can't allow itself to relax, laugh, and be careless. Freud's "classic" formulation of paranoia was itself a kind of paranoia: an attempt to explain a whole complex area of experience by means of the tightest, most contorted and introverted logic. For Freud, paranoia was a screen over homosexual desires and fears, and his ingenious formulation was used to support his pansexual theory of human behavior. "I love him, but it is forbidden to love a male, therefore I hate him. But I must have a reason for hating him, therefore I hate him because he persecutes me." It went something like that.

But modern psychoanalysis has itself moved further and further away from Freud's view, so there is no point in our engaging and repeating a dispute that is now largely settling itself. What I want to do instead, in this brief essay, is to give the main dimensions for understanding paranoia so that we can see it in all its complexity and simplicity at the same time. In this way any student of man, or anyone who reflects on himself, can go straight to the matter without having to redigest and try to pull together the enormous volume of good and mostly bad writing on this problem.

The first thing to be said, in all seriousness, is that everyone is paranoid at one time or other—if he has any sensitivity at all. And in our modern world one mild paranoid fantasy per week would be about par for the average person; and to have no paranoid fantasies at all, ever, should certainly mark one off as an uninteresting clod. In a word, paranoia comes easiest to those who are open to the fine shades of experience, to the lopsidedness of the world, the miscarriages of events, the undercurrent of hopelessness of the human condition.

The first general dimension in which paranoia has to be cogitated is what we can call the Personal-Power Dimension. To convey it, let us take a simple hypothetical example of how two people might view the same situation. Take, on the one hand, the man who feels on top of things as he steps out of his house on the way to work in the morning. As he opens the door a car with two men in it pulls away from the curb. Since our man is confident that he belongs in an ordered world where rational people go about their business, independently and responsibly, he would probably not notice the car at all, or even the fact that one of its occupants glanced at him. And if he did notice it, he would probably pay it no mind; he feels the security of his own presence, the basic solidity and meaningfulness of his own life. On the other hand, let us take a second man on his way to work who similarly steps out of his door and sees the same scene, but whose presence in the world is wholly different. This man is uneasy about his job, his relationship to his wife, the future of his small children in an unfriendly world. He feels generally insignificant, helpless, overwhelmed by events. His pattern of perception, then, would be quite different. The timing of the car pulling away from the curb would be too exact to be a coincidence; the casual glance of the man in the car on the curbside would be converted to a knowing, measuring glance. "Was that a notebook in his hand? Did he look past me as I opened the door, and see my wife in her negligee? What is going on—what are they planning? What fate is in store for me and my loved ones?"

The paranoid fantasy builds on one's insecure power base, his helplessness in the world, his inability to take command of his experience, to get on top of the evil in the world. Here is the nub of the matter. One feels overwhelmed and has to make sense out of his precarious position. And the way to do this is to attribute *definite* motives to *definite* people. This seems to straighten the situation out, to put one back into things. There is now a focus, a center, with lines running from others to oneself and to one's objects and loved ones. There is something one can *do* from his position of utter helplessness: he can go back in for a second cup of coffee, and wait a few minutes to see if anyone comes; he can leave instructions not to let the children play in front of the house for a few days; he can make sure the door is securely locked when he leaves; he can come home from work early, possibly to catch someone unexpectedly in his bed—and so on, and on. And even if he can't do anything, or especially if he can't do anything, at least he can order the world in his thought, see and make connections between things that are so unconnected; he can put concern back into a world in which there is so little concern. And above all, he masks his feelings of impotence in the face of events; his helplessness is now no longer his own tragic shortcoming, but a realistic reaction to the real actions of others. Furthermore, he is someone to reckon with: he recently bought a gun.

We might call this "existential" paranoia, the reactions to one's smallness and finitude in this awesome universe. The

hypothetical example above is simple enough, taken from everyday experience, but more complex examples are even more
instructive. They show how natural is the existential paranoid
reaction when the individual is overextended from his power
base. I am thinking of a film story which played some time
back, starring Michèle Morgan in the role of a dutiful, middle-
class wife. Her husband was an uninteresting and unimaginative
plodder, a pinched, ungenerous man. Michèle Morgan had her
usual attractive qualities: tall and straight, head held back and
high; her manner was quiet and straightforward, and her person gave the suggestion of a strong and deep interior life—the
locus of fathomless subjectivity and proud natural strength that
men everywhere seek in women. But aside from that, and except
for a sensitive and generous nature, she was the middle-class
equal of her husband. Besides, she was not particularly good
looking, being possessed of a thick, high-bridged nose. The crux
of the story is that she meets an altruistic plastic surgeon who
draws her a sketch of how she would look after a simple cos-
metic operation on her nose. Of course, she is struck with the
idea of so easily overcoming her plainness, and thinks her
husband would be overjoyed to have a wife like the one in the
sketch, a classic Athenian beauty in place of the standard Pari-
sian suburban vintage. Imagine everyone's surprise when the
husband greets this opportunity with a fit of rage, and will
have none of this nonsense.

Then the story moves to a quick and relentless *dénouement*.
She goes ahead with the operation, thinking to surprise and
overcome him with a *fait accompli*. And from this point on

their lives change and their marriage disintegrates. He becomes paranoidly jealous of the plastic surgeon, and after the most violent and gratuitous quarrels with his wife, he succeeds in driving her into the arms of the surgeon. In all this the wife understands nothing of what has happened, why the most generous gesture on her part has turned her husband into a maniacal enemy, why their life together must now end. The film itself ends, if I recall correctly, in the husband's killing the surgeon.

It requires no great imagination to understand what the wife could not: the paranoia of her plodding husband. It was simply that he did not have enough of a secure footing in the world, a confident power base, with which to support the burden of a truly breathtaking wife. It was too much for him; it upset the delicate esthetic balance of his middle-class life, put a burden of uniqueness and unaccustomedness onto him, made him responsible for dealing with an object that was too much out of the ordinary, cast too much of an aura, drew too much attention to itself. The husband's feeling of being overwhelmed was translated into an attempt to make sense out of a suddenly upsetting world. Everything vaguely helpless in himself was given fixed points in other people: the unfaithful wife, the plotting surgeon. The paranoid delusion gives his world form, but a rigid and false form that destroys it. The moral of the story is that *Homo sapiens* is an animal who is fated to seek the causes and interrelationships of things, and if he reads them entirely in the wrong place, it brings his world down around his shoulders. This is a moral not only for jealous husbands with beautiful wives, but also and especially for leaders and law-makers of great nations.

When we ponder this example we can understand that the existential paranoia that results from being overextended from one's power base can be a reaction to a life that goes out of balance for any number of reasons: not only beautiful wives, but also sumptuous homes, stables of luxurious cars, a yacht —or any sudden fulfillment of an impossible life dream. The person is literally overwhelmed by the object, cannot support its superlativeness with his meager ordinariness. Freud got at this kind of thing beautifully with his insights into the "wrecked by success" syndrome: a man gradually builds a career and finally climbs the coveted last rung to the highest achievement— only to go to pieces and lose everything, including his sanity sometimes. As very often with Freud, he gave us the richest insights, but explained them with the wrong reasons. He under-stood the "wrecked by success" syndrome as a problem of the classic Oedipus complex: the son succeeds by surpassing the father, and his life disintegrates because this is the one com-mand that he dare not transgress. To surpass the father re-awakens the primary guilt of the Oedipal competition, the desire to kill the father and copulate with the mother. This is the guilt the successful person cannot stand.

But Freud himself, unlike many of his disciples, was a grow-ing man, and very late in life he wrote a revealing self-analytic paper titled "A Disturbance of Memory on the Acropolis." As I noted elsewhere (1968, p. 400), in this paper Freud did not talk crassly about the Oedipus, about patricidal fears and competition for the mother. When it came to explaining one of his own long-standing neurotic troubles, he understood it finally as an unwillingness to surpass his father because of *piety* for him. Freud had come so far from the simple rigidity of his own pet formulations that it would seem ungrateful for us to accuse him of not taking the next step—a step, we might say, to the side of his early disciple Alfred Adler. Then he would have understood what seems to me to be at the base not only of the neurotic troubles he described in this important late paper, but at the base of his whole life style: I mean that instead of talking about piety for the father, he should have frankly admitted that in his new experiences he no longer had his father as a *secure power base*. To be wrecked by success is to be undermined by the inability to support the grandiose superstructure of a plentiful life on the foundations of one's helpless aloneness and finitude. If I were asked for the single most striking insight into human nature and the human condition, it would be this: that no person is strong enough to support the meaning of his life unaided by something outside him. But this is the last thing the individual will admit to himself, because to admit it means to break away the armored mask of righteous self-assurance that surrounds his whole life-striving. And it is just this that would push hi n to the brink of desperation and disintegration. To drop the pretense of self-sufficiency is to destroy the laboriously built-up social self; and if we destroy it we must build an entirely new one, on entirely new foundations of meaning and self-worth. It is because Kierkegaard understood this that I would rank him as a greater psychologist than Freud.

If we approach the "wrecked by success" problem along these lines, we should also have to restudy a whole range of phenomena that seem unrelated, but that really take root in the same problem. Pregnancy and postpartum reactions in women, who suddenly find themselves no longer their mother's child but a mother on their own, with all the separateness and responsibility that this entails. They no longer stand firmly on someone else's power base, but must now *be* a power base of their own. "Nervous breakdowns" of adolescents who win unexpectedly high honors, and young people on the eve of their marriage or honeymoon, also fall into this category. We would be especially rewarded with new understanding if we overhauled our whole study of what the psychoanalysts so glibly call "homosexual panics." Not only would we see that in most cases a homosexual panic is not a homosexual panic, but we would also get a glimpse of one of the ideal solutions for the universal problem of individual weakness. Let us dwell on this for a moment because it sums up so much of what we are discussing.

The idea of a homosexual panic drew its credibility—of course—from the psychoanalytic pansexual theory that was used to explain it. Children, in this view, are "polymorphous perverse" organisms—they combine elements of sexuality from both sexes, and in their urge for total stimulation and gratification, would secretly want to play the role of both sexes. But in growing up, during the Oedipal crisis, they have to fix on one role and abandon the other; but the wish for both the mother and the father is buried deep in the unconscious. The homosexual panic of the male adult, is a recognition and a fear

[131]

of this secret wish, this forbidden desire to play the passive partner of the father. This is, roughly, the psychoanalytic view, and it does have some truth in it—but again, for the wrong reasons. The male child does like to snuggle, he may enjoy stimulating himself by rubbing himself in the father's lap; his highest delight might be to merge himself in the warm protectiveness of the father's barrel chest and feel the waves of comforting power and security throb through him in the father's deep voice. But this is not because the child has a sexual-instinctive make-up that determines his wishes and his fate, but rather, as we shall want to remind ourselves again, because as a living organism he seeks to merge himself in the aura of superior power. Even the extreme opposite situation can be explained equally in gross power motives, and not narrowly sexual ones: I mean the young man whose father was weak and effeminate, and who did not give him a solid model for a straightforward male role. The bankruptcy of the son's feelings of power and adequacy would be even more pronounced, and his maleness might be in doubt his whole life long.

Here we have two kinds of simple and straightforward explanations—the Freudian one, and what we might call the Adlerian one. But it is not easy to persuade people that the open Adlerian explanation is preferable to the hidden Freudian one. The Freudian approach seems "more scientific" to many minds because it seems to get at exact and precise physical facts, instead of global, imprecise ones. No less a humanist psychologist than Abraham Maslow, for example, when he was studying the behavior of baboons, gave undue credence to Freud. He saw that males preserve themselves by inviting coitus with a stronger male, rather than by fighting. Maslow thought that we might share this instinctive, passive homosexuality with our subhuman cousins: that we might tend to confuse our instinctive sexual needs with our own identity needs—and thus, the homosexual panic in adults. And he cites as possible evidence a patient in such a panic who ran away from his wife and hid in a hotel room in another city. He was frightened and couldn't sleep, when suddenly, during the night as he lay in bed on his back he felt the weight of a presence on top of him. He submitted to it lovingly and felt "This is God." He felt peaceful and slept deeply for the first time in months. Next morning, he awoke refreshed and relaxed and determined to serve God by his good works, which he now does. He returned to his wife and is heterosexual with her.

When I cited this illustration in a previous writing (1962, p. 181), I warned about the danger of this kind of speculation, of confounding primate instincts and human problems. Today I would be even more firm: there is absolutely no evidence for this fanciful speculation. We can phrase our confusions in human terms and make more sense out of them than if we phrase them in baboon terms; and even if we can't rig up a "real scientific-looking study" by watching animals mate in their natural habitat, we can be even more truthful and empirical. The fact is that the problem of identity is a problem of strength: one has to feel that he has the power to put forth a consistent maleness—and all families do not provide the child with the backgrounds for earning this sense of power. Even if the patient were to phrase his fears in homosexual language, or allow the psychiatrist to phrase them that way, we would still have to be suspicious: we know that sex-language is a ready shorthand that sums up one's personal helplessness: "Yes, I'm so confused, I feel drawn to that man's powerful presence, so overcome by strange anxieties when I am with women," etc. This is not a baboon talking, but a weak and confused adult, who does not feel the plenitude of his own secure presence.

And now we can draw the circle on our discussion. What Maslow's example really shows is that we do share one thing with the baboons, the same thing we share with all herd-animal life: the utter anxiety of our finitude, our lifelong urge to drown our feelings of helplessness and inadequacy in some self-transcending source of sure power. *This* is what we can safely say is the "animal" in us, and it makes us the kin not only of baboons but of horses, dogs, buffaloes, and sea lions. The difficulty of man's situation is that he does not have the easy way out of his subhuman cousins: when he feels his powerlessness he has to search to overcome it. And it is precisely here, as we promised, that we get a glimpse of one of the ideal solutions for this basic human problem. We can now see that Maslow's patient used good intuitive sense in resolving his dilemma of identity and power. He gave himself frankly over to a merger with the ultimate power base available to man. This is how we have come to understand the primary role of the religious experience in mental illness, from the great work of Kierkegaard through William James and on up to the courageous honesty of Anton Boisen. Boisen frankly showed, through his own experiences, that our understanding of mental illness cannot be allowed to stop short of the problem of the ultimate power source in which to ground one's life. The recognition of one's finitude, and his dependence on outside sources of power to sustain him, may be ideally answered by frankly throwing oneself at the mercy of the Lord of Creation. If one can do this honestly, from within his total experience, he makes a perfect closure on his growth without bringing it to an end or compromising his freedom. When all is said and done, the difference between "sick" and "healthy" religion is a matter of whether one resolves his power problem in an open, free, critical way, or in a desperate, reflexive, deterministic way. Here there is no need to argue about how "true" this solution is: truth for man is relative, and the ideal by which to measure it must always be the standard of openness, growth, and continuing freedom for the developing life. If the choice is set against these standards, then it is "true," the only meaningful truth that organisms can know. When we ponder these simple facts we can see why our understanding of the ideal solution to the problem of man's powerlessness is still more or less where Epictetus left it over two thousand years ago:

> ". . . what else can I do, a lame old man, but sing hymns to God? Were I a nightingale, I would act the part of a nightingale; were I a swan, the part of a swan. But since I am a reasonable creature, it is my duty to praise God . . . and I call on you to join the same song."

What he is saying is that in a world of organisms, where power is limited, the reasonable thing to do is to find the real and best source. And the difference between man and animals is really a difference in opportunity, not in limitation.

II.

So much, then, for the Personal-Power Dimension of the problem of paranoia. The next large dimension of the spectrum on paranoia is perhaps even more interesting; and it is, like the first dimension, universal to our present human condition. We might call it the Historical-Psychological Dimension. It is summed up in the great change that has taken place in our *perception* of the world: in all the many ways that the world has sharply altered, none is more striking than the way it has altered in our perception of it. For over a million years—probably as long ago as human life had evolved, man saw the world in one general way. Then, beginning with the Greeks and more sharply since Newton, we have come to see it in a quite radically different way. It would be impossible to overstress the importance of this change in perception. For one thing, it contributed to our greater freedom from natural forces; and for another, it led to our almost complete impoverishment and strangeness in the universe. Many writers have written about it and occasionally it is briefly touched upon in an anthropology course. In view of its importance I simply do not understand why it is not made a required and central part of one's intellectual experience in college.

Primitive and archaic man lived in a universe that was alive, moral, and personal. It was a "Thou" world, not an "It" world, and it was not a Thou set off over and against man, but a Thou in which he was literally immersed. Every one of man's important acts took on a moral, personal quality, in a universe that was mysteriously alive: trees, rocks, wind, clouds, everything could be loaded with awesome splendor and intense meaning. It was Chesterton who taught us beautifully how to imagine the kind of world the primitive sees: we have only to imagine ourselves suddenly placed in Times Square, at night, with the gigantic neons in flashing movement and color—*without being able to read*, and *without knowing that things can move without being alive*. And it was G. Van der Leeuw, above all, in his great work *Religion in Essence and Manifestation*, who taught us conclusively how intensely personal such a world was. Somewhere he quotes a Navaho Indian protesting his sincerity:

> "Why should I lie to you? I am ashamed before the earth: I am ashamed before the heavens: I am ashamed before the dawn: I am ashamed before the blue sky: I am ashamed before the darkness: I am ashamed before the sun: I am ashamed before that standing within me which speaks with me. I am never out of sight; therefore I must tell the truth. I hold my word tight in my breast."

And we have the same primitivity in the Bible, where the Psalmist says:

> "Lord, you said: seek you my face: your face Lord I do seek."

The world of primitive and archaic man, in a word, was a moral arena of faces and fates. Persons, gods, and spiritual beings of all kinds *caused* things to happen; nothing was casual or abstracted.

There is no point in my going over this vast literature here, and saying at secondhand what Lévy-Bruhl, G. Van der Leeuw, Henri Frankfort, F. M. Cornford, Mircea Eliade, Robert Redfield, and others have said so well. The thing I want to stress is that all this was lost and has changed. The change all started with the Greek philosophers, especially Democritus, whose famous atomic theory was a major blow aimed at the universe of personal spirits: he wanted to show that all is matter and the void, and thereby quiet the terrible anxiousness of his contemporaries, who saw spirits and personal meaning in the natural events around them. Newton finished the job that Democritus began, and gave us a completely material, mechanized world, utterly abstracted, utterly devoid of personal significance to us, emptied of spiritual qualities. Even God's face was pushed way into the background. This too is familiar history, we know the freedom and the power over the natural order that this change in viewpoint gave us. But now let us dwell for a minute on the toll of this change because here is where it illuminates our understanding of paranoia.

The simple fact is that we live in an impersonal world, but the more sensitive among us *do not like it.* After all, what bothers us most about our strange career on this planet is that our lives are subject to complete catastrophe by the simplest accident, the merest chance occurrence. This is the thing we can't stand. The undoing of years of work, effort, good will, morality, patience, sacrifice—by one tiny random event: the prick by a dirty needle in a simple hospital check-up; one moment of inattention on a routine drive that we have made a thousand times; a leaky gas jet in a brand-new heater—the examples are thousandfold, and each one more disgusting than the next. Disgusting is the apt word for randomness, for meaningless mechanical accident that takes such a heavy toll of beautifully live and pulsating, complex natural organisms. But primitive man was not disgusted about chance because nothing happened randomly: if there was an evil event, it was because *someone* willed it. Those among us who protest against the impersonality of their world are really trying primitively to banish some of its senselessness. This is why even a hardheaded scientist like Wilhelm Reich could congratulate himself on *growing into* a more primitive view of reality; he knew that if you take personal significance out of the world, you impoverish it and make yourself a stranger in it. This too is why, at bottom we all like gossip: we all love a personal world, we revel in faces and fates, in earthly careers, we want to know what happened to Mr. Jones's *organism* and his face, his operations, how he is wrinkling, what his worries are, whom he married and whether she is beautiful, whether she nags. We don't care about his latest publication, his bright idea, or his new suit. The depersonalization of causality and of man's fate might do for the academic intellectuals who hire out their abstracted intellects to the war machines, and for our Secretaries of Defense who calculate human deaths in numbers of "only one hundred million" dead. No primitive could think this way, and neither can the sensitive person today.

And this is the heart of much paranoia for the sensitive soul: he can't stand the impersonality of evil. He wants motives and living power behind the fateful events. This is the meaning of much of the deep stirring about the Garrison investigation of Kennedy's assassination and of the rumors about the CIA and the FBI (one that I recently heard is that "they" have a way of inducing heart attacks in undesirable but prominent people, so that death looks natural). The point is that we simply cannot allow ourselves to believe in and to live with disinterested, bureaucratic evil. This explains too the shocked reaction of many people to Hannah Arendt's view of Eichmann: it is just too much to believe that simple bureaucratic decision, simple paper-work expediency, can abstractedly grind up six million lives. The rape of entire nations and peoples, the explosion of nuclear weapons, the spreading of chemicals, gas, and germs—surely this cannot be a mere matter of double-entry bookkeeping, of standard office memoranda, of "doing good" in the organization according to the daily program for efficient operation—and then knocking off for a martini and lunch. Somewhere behind it, somehow, there must be an evil will; and in the daily operations there must be a multitude of conniving and evil people. So we would like to think. And so we draw the caricatures of our political figures, to make them loom deeper, larger and more portentous than the simple empty trimmers and rubber-stampers that they might really be.

The dread of the paranoid and of modern man draws from the same source: evil must happen because somebody *cares*. And if you can find the somebody, and finger him, then your powers are not without effect in the world. Psychology teaches us how paranoia is an attempt to overcome powerlessness; and historical psychology shows us how this powerlessness has been

accentuated in modern times. We should not wonder that everyone is so jumpy, that occasionally someone takes to a tower with
a rifle, to survey a landscape where evil is definable and can be
located in real bodies, which can then be quickly dispatched.
We should not wonder that the men who run the vast computer
machine of modern bureaucracy everywhere see plots by foreign
agents, by a world communist movement, by evil *persons*. Even
the empty abstractors have to breathe meaning into their
Frankenstein monster. It can't be permitted that units in space,
numbers, papers, and tubes, be the masters of man's fate.

And so we can conclude that the Dimension of Historical-
Psychology teaches us how much mental illness is a matter of
our social institutions and our social and intellectual history.
The attempt by Democritus and Newton to quiet our fears
and give us back our dispossessed world has only served to
make us feel even more dispossessed—and we are right back
where we started, just as frightened and crazy as people were
at the disintegration of the Ancient and the Medieval worlds.
Fortunately, some psychiatrists are beginning to talk about the
importance of the problem of meaning in mental illness, and are
no longer looking with scorn at the priests. The problem of
man in society today is exactly at the point where Judeo-Christianity picked it up at the demise of the Ancient world: namely,
how to give back to each individual life the deep sense that it
had *universal moral significance*.[1]

III.

The final dimension that we have to consider in order to get
a complete spectrum on the problem of paranoia is more subtle

and perhaps more interesting than the first two. It is the Esthetic or Dramatistic Dimension in the strict sense of the word. It reflects the discrepancy between one's feelings of his own worth and the picture that the world reflects of that worth. Man is the animal who lives on words and images; his whole life is a dramatistic performance, a symbolic edifice that gives him his sense of value. In a word, his value is *staged*. And so his very life blood is caught up in the symbolic staging. When the world reflects a lesser image than he has worked toward and thinks he has created or otherwise deserves deep down, then there is a need for esthetic reordering. Paranoid fantasy is a principal device for righting the imbalance, for warding off the invasion of meaninglessness into a life that feels it has achieved so much that ought to be meaningful.

The one who has the most trouble with this problem is, as we might expect, the creative genius. He is caught in the terrible bind of presenting to the world a magnificent edifice testifying to his true greatness—only to have the world turn its back on him in incomprehension, fear, or derision. The thing is so usual with real works of genius that it almost represents a law of history, and even the popular mind is familiar with it, and knows it to be an injustice. I have recently written quite a bit on this problem in *The Structure of Evil,* especially in reference to Rousseau, but touching also on others, like Herman Melville. So there is no point in repeating my discussion of the creative innovator here.[2] What I do want to talk about briefly is how this Dramatistic Dimension touches the heart of the lives of every one of us, from the average man on the street to the ruler of states.

Take the average man who has to stage in his own way the life drama of his own worth and significance. As a youth he, like everyone else, feels that deep down he has a special talent, an indefinable but real something to contribute to the richness and success of Life in the Universe. But, like almost everyone else, he doesn't seem to hit on the unfolding of this special something; his life takes on the character of a series of accidents and encounters that carry him along, willy-nilly, into new experiences and responsibilities. Career, marriage, family, approaching old age—all these *happen* to him, he doesn't command them. Instead of his staging a drama of his own significance, he himself is staged, programmed by the standard scenario laid down by his society. He is carried through the production by the accidents of fate and fortune, and only inserts his will into it by accepting to sweat with his brow and assume responsibility for the situations he moves into. I am not implying that this is ugly or undignified: it is probably the highest heroism. The only thing is that it is not *his* drama. As often happens a man or woman may live to see the best of their efforts to salvage some kind of decent performance go to naught. In middle age one might see his children go to jail or die pointlessly in an auto accident or fraternity house fire; his wife become an alcoholic, an adultress, or just a mindless, nagging hag. And to cap it all, it might gradually become plain to him that the company to which he has given his best talents and energies in the job into which he stumbled in his youth, could always have gotten along really without him. In other words, he gradually comes to feel that he has made no contribution to world life.

Poets and playwrights who give us a *Krapp's Last Tape*, a *Death of a Salesman* or a *Come Back Little Sheba* show us how well they understand this problem, and how close it is to all of us. And Jung has written some of his most excellent things about the crisis of middle age, of life after forty, which sums up the task that also befalls us all. In a sense all of our lives "fail" to be what we once felt they might be; and even if we succeed by worldly standards, our real success is never sure: there is always something unconvincing and unsubstantial about even the most exemplary life drama. We may be led to compare it to the vast panorama of evolution, the rise and fall of whole civilizations, the countless numbers of human bones and skulls that make a graveyard of this planet—the imminence of absolute and complete catastrophe that could wipe away in a minute the whole career of evolution—and seemingly, the whole worth and value of the destiny of humanity. So Jung could well say that we are all tasked, at some point in our advancing age, to reassess the meaning of our whole lives in terms of the largest, most self-transcending meanings. And only in this way could we hope to put some kind of reasonable, self-satisfying ending on the fragile drama of our individual fates.

If we do not or cannot make some fortunate and heroic re-conceptualization of the meaning of human life, then we have to try, in some way, to make sense out of a drama that has been botched. Those who are the most desperate and the most help-less are forced to invent paranoid languages to justify their failure: languages of jealousy delusions that accuse their spouses; languages of guilt delusions that accuse themselves;

languages of hate that accuse their children, their friends, and their employers (see Becker, 1964). These are desperate *intellectual devices* that attempt to make sense out of lives that have bogged down and failed. More usually, and for most of us, the reaction is to tighten up, insist on how right we have always been anyway, how good our efforts have been, how correct the old models and the old standards—standards to which people "nowadays" no longer adhere, and so on. "It is not we who have failed, it is the world, and the quality of people in it. The drama we have staged is all right; it is the world in which we have staged it that makes it seem all wrong." This is the more usual reaction, as we said, it is the reaction that most young people see all around them. And with the intuitive genius of youth they have coined the proper condemnation of these salvaging efforts: they see that most people over thirty-five are "up-tight." But they don't understand what is at stake in this tightness, since they do not yet have a finished life drama that has to be justified. Since they are still growing they can't know how difficult it is to grow into a new world conceptualization after forty. The character armor they see is the middle way for the masses of men: the slim and lucky possibility of new growth, on one side; the breakdown in the face of meaninglessness, on the other. And for man, as we know, new growth only takes place in the teeth of breakdown. This is why character armor is a reasonable and benign way out. It is the same broad path that the new generation will itself, in the main, have to follow to keep its balance as dramatists working with the impoverished means of a human existence.

So much, then, for the esthetic problems of the average man. Let us look finally at a different kind of curse, in the man who seems most fortunate: I mean the one who has all the means at his disposal for the complete staging of the drama of his own significance—the absolute ruler. If it seems like the average man has an impossible life task, the dilemma of the "chosen ones" is even more fateful and remorseless. It drives home again and finally the lesson that there is no royal road out of the limitations of the human condition.

Offhand we might imagine that the ideal thing for man would be to be able to control all the props and performers in his life plot. Yet when we glance over history we see just the opposite: the careers of most of those who held absolute power were corrupted, destroyed, or somehow cheated by that power. The famous dictum that comes immediately to mind is Acton's: "Power corrupts, and absolute power corrupts absolutely." The dictum is now a commonplace, but what is not commonplace is the psychological reason for most of the corruption of absolute power. It works something like this: The absolute leader has the power to stage the drama of his own significance, he can almost completely order the performance world immediately around him and wherever he travels. This kind of drama provides him with a sure reflection of his own greatness and infallibility; everyone joins in to fill flawlessly the roles that the staging requires: counselor, minister, priest, soldier, peasant, mistress—single personalities in the foreground, ranks and ranks of uniformed ones in the background. As long as everyone performs as they are supposed to, the ruler can have no idea that he is not the perfect one for the part, the chosen one of time, fate, and the gods. We immediately think of Jean Genet's *The Balcony* as the modern genial insight into this aspect of the human tragedy. The point is that man is a dramatistic animal, and he himself gets caught up in the staging. The performance acquires its own esthetic integrity and begins to use for its own purposes its own central character. He is put in the position of not being able to stand any esthetic discrepancies between his own feeling of worth and the image that the drama reflects of him. He has to balance and juggle, and perform and direct all the harder. He has to be as great and infallible as the plot shows him to be. This is the fatal circularity in which he is caught: the fact that he *can* make the world reflect the image of his greatness *obliges* him to do so, since the one thing that man cannot stand, as we said, is the discordancy between what he feels is true, and what the world reflects as true. As the world exaggerates his feelings of unusual worth, he then has to further support and stage the exaggeration. He ends up caught in his own fictional staging, and may be forced to try to prove it real in more and more of its discordant details. And so we have the "natural" unfolding of megalomanic paranoia that has taken such a monstrous toll all through human history.[3] The ruler literally feeds human life into the drama of his own importance. The average subject is at best only a potential prop for the ruler's dramatistic needs; at worst, he is a potential hindrance or interference with the image the ruler has to maintain. In former times whole nations could be jerked about by the bad digestion of a king or the sex fantasies of a queen.

In our time we have seen the famous purge trials by Stalin and the fantastic military blunders by Hitler in the Russian campaign, when he just had to see things come out the way he wanted them. The examples are numberless. We have even caught a glimpse of this psychology in our own troubled democracy, as we watched Lyndon Johnson get caught up in a war that he had to prove was esthetically correct, and that had to reflect the proper image of his rightness and infallibility. He had to be careful about details of the staging of this drama of his rightness, even to the extent of avoiding churches where antagonistic sermons might be preached at him: FBI men went out beforehand and checked on the minister's views and allegiances. When the President traveled, it was more and more to military installations where he could see immediately reflected the plot that he was in, and not risk seeing any other kind of scenario.

When the modern ideal of democracy was forged in the teeth of the tyranny of European monarchy, the theorists understood these things very well. Our President's fault was that his office had been allowed to accrue too much power. The founding fathers of our country saw that unchecked power was a trap even for the most well-intentioned person; they understood that it was the duty of his fellows to help him avoid that trap by making it impossible for him to use that power for purely personal needs. The leaders never know it, but they need the perspectives of the people—not because these people elected them to office, but in order to keep their sanity and balance once they get there. The ancients knew it too, which I think is the key to the saying "Whom the gods would destroy they first make mad." All the gods have to do is to give a man an exaggerated idea of his own importance, and the power and means to stage that idea—and he will accomplish the necessary self-destruction. The ancients, who were more philosophical and worldly wise than we are, knew that it is simply not possible for man to order the world to his own design, or to justify the value of his own life. This must come from beyond. The ancients had not lost, as we have, the sense that man lives in two worlds, the unknown one from which he came, and the "fallen" one in which he performs the pathetic drama of his self-justification. They understood, then, that man's tragedy is that he is in and of this world, not the "more perfect" one. And so his sense of value is tied to earthly and vanishing things, as he himself is earthly and vanishing. For such a poor creature, in sum, there can be no perfect esthetic apotheosis. He is a performer in Someone Else's still unknown production, and not the producer of his own. All of which brings us back to Epictetus's wise words: it is not man's calling to be praised, but to praise.

IV.

There is one important conclusion that I want to draw from this brief overview. We have sketched three perspectives or dimensions of the problem of paranoia, and now we can better understand that they all center on one basic problem: the problem of the forward-momentum of an organismic life, a momentum that is at all times basically biological, but at all times symbolically potentiated and mediated. Paranoia is truly a kind of poetics, a weaving of images around the limitations of the human situation, the plight of a peculiarly limited organism. And so we can understand the difference between rich poetics and poor ones. Rich poetics take in a totality of experience that includes pulsating organisms *and* airy symbols. They are based on a depth of physical feeling and they draw on a richness of total experience. Poor poetics draw on shallow emotions and thin feeling, on impoverished organisms—in a word, on symbolic superstructures without sure foundations.

The lesson that paranoia teaches us is the same one we learn from all the "mental" confusions—schizophrenia, depression, the perversions: they all seem to be problems in "thought," but they are really problems of a *total life lived*. Cognition of any kind is itself a reflection of the situation of the whole organism. And so, the best thoughts, as we know, derive from the richest experience, from one's whole situation in the world. If you are at ease, comfortable, feel you belong, sense the plenitude of your powers—then your thoughts are generous, warm, broad, rich, tentative, and open. If you are cramped, trapped, weak, overwhelmed, *underneath* your experience—then your thoughts are mean, chilly, poor, humorless, dogmatic, and closed. Mental patients almost always say "my mind is confused, something is wrong in my head." That's where the symptoms are, but not the problem. The patient does not know that the kind of thinking you do depends on the seating of your whole body and being in the world.

The problem of mental health, then, is always fundamentally

a problem of organisms which are crippled, cramped, or blocked in their experience. This is what we have learned from the long development of psychotherapy: that intellectual insight alone is not enough for personality change and personal freedom. The psychotherapist talks about the need for "emotional insight" and "emotional catharsis," in addition to intellectual growth. But these are clumsy words that really obscure the main problem. What the patient needs is to immerse himself in a long and total growth experience. This alone gives him the possibility of inner or "emotional" change. When we talk about "emotional" growth we are talking about the forward-momentum of the total organism, moving beyond its constricting problems. This is always both cognitive and physical, a growth of liberating perspectives of the mind, and of inner mellowing of the body. This is one reason that psychotherapy has such a poor record of success: because it cannot substitute for a whole life lived. It is not enough to "find out" the trouble one is in, or to "straighten out" his confused thoughts. Once you find what is wrong you are still saddled with the immense task of changing your whole organismic seating in the world. To aim for sanity is to aim for the long slow growth of one's powers and sensitivities in the real world of experience. This is what John Dewey, perhaps above all others, understood so well; it is the basis for his whole philosophy of progressive education. This, too, is what the writings of Wilhelm Reich and Norman O. Brown are about: they are a Rousseauian plea for total organismic experience as the basis for real sanity. When we think of the problem in these total mind-body terms, we can understand, too, why Eastern philosophy is just as modern as any other for the problems of personality growth and change: it deals with the seating of the organism in the world, with relaxing it, steadying it, mellowing it, placing it under one's free and easy control, deepening it in its inner dimensions, making it a repository of rich, multidimensional experiences.

In sum, then, to talk about a sane society is to talk about a world that loves and respects the noise and laughter of swarming children and galloping adolescents, a world that values pulsating life over mechanical things, whole organisms—minds in bodies—over part truths, new birth over old interests. Most of all, our brief survey of the problem of paranoia reveals that no amount of frenzied thought or logic can give us these wholesome values. They can only come about by a broad, comprehensive effort by modern man to refind himself in the universe, to triumph over the modern dilemma of his strangeness on this earth. He has to rewin his sense of trust, his mellowness of mood, his relaxedness and belongingness. He must overcome the feeling that throws such a dismal shadow over him: that he is an accident, his life a whim, his face alien, his efforts unwanted and unneeded. The only way to do this, as the Personalist philosophers have so well understood, is to win back a conviction that man has a career and a destiny on this planet, a destiny which will somehow make its mark and contribute its share to the life of the whole universe. *This* is the "psychiatric" problem.

SUMMER, 1968

Notes

1. The "Personalist" school of philosophy, of which Mounier was such a prominent representative, is part of the modern answer to this problem.

2. I don't want here either to broach or dwell on the argument between the psychoanalytic view of the mental troubles of, say, a Melville, and the esthetic view of these troubles that I share with some literary critics. For those who are already familiar with the argument the only thing that has to be settled—and it is very simple—is this: Which approach *includes* the other? The reductionist approach that talks about Melville's relation to his mother, his early childhood training and environment that made his organism so precariously seated in the world, does partly explain Melville's reactions to his adult experiences—but it does not simply include them or cause them. His reaction to the esthetic discrepancy between his great work *Moby Dick,* and the world's reception of that work during his lifetime, *does* include the reductionist explanation, and largely absorbs it. Had the world reacted differently he would probably not have experienced the neurotic troubles on which the psychoanalytic approach is based. And so, the one approach is better than the other. All the more so, in fact, because it was precisely his personal discomfort, the underside of homelessness, that was the urge to his talent and genius. If he had had a childhood that was psychoanalytically beyond reproach we should never know his name. When are psychoanalysts going to begin gracefully to accept these simple facts? Perhaps only when they relinquish their total claim on man, and are willing to accept a more modest place as a part of our approach to human failure. But this would raise havoc with the aura of infallibility that surrounds their private practice—and here is where the problem really lies, and what makes it so recalcitrant.

The interested reader should compare a psychoanalytic document on this case, with a literary one. For example, see Charles Kligerman's partly relevant and partly alarming and ludicrous essay "The Psychology of Herman Melville" in the *Psychoanalytic Review,* Vol. 40, 1953, pp. 125–43; and compare it to Richard Chase's *Herman Melville: A Critical Study* (New York: Macmillan, 1949).

3. Lewis Mumford has understood how central to tyranny of all kinds, is this problem of the symbolic fabrication of human worth, and the social staging of it. See his major work of historical psychology in this half of the century: *The Myth of the Machine: Technics and Human Development* (New York: Harcourt, Brace and World, 1966).

References

Becker, E. (1962), *The Birth and Death of Meaning: A Perspective in Psychiatry and Anthropology* (New York: Free Press).

——. (1964), *The Revolution in Psychiatry: The New Understanding of Man* (New York: Free Press).

——. (1968), *The Structure of Evil: An Essay on the Unification of the Science of Man* (New York: Braziller).

Chesterton, G. K. (1908), *Orthodoxy* (New York: Image Books, 1959).

VI | WHAT IS *BASIC* HUMAN NATURE?

Further Notes on the Central
Problem of the Science of Man

One must always tell what one sees.
Above all, which is more difficult,
one must always see what one sees.
                                    CHARLES PÉGUY

. . . but what is one to do in a country
in which "safety" is the one principle
used to settle intellectual matters?
                                    WILLIAM JAMES

The problem of whether man is basically "good," "evil," or simply "neutral" is central to the Science of Man. And the reason that it is central is simply this: the shape of our science must be largely influenced by the Image of Man at its center. Say that man is good—and you have one kind of social theory; say that he is bad—and you have a philosophy that more or less determines how you will formulate your hypotheses about man and society.

We might imagine that a question so crucial to the cast of a whole science would be one on which there would be some large agreement after some two thousand years of the best human thought. Or, wanting such agreement, we might imagine that there would be heated argument on platforms, in research laboratories, in high schools and colleges—and hopefully, perhaps even in our legislative and governing councils. Or, finally, wanting this heated debate, we might imagine that the reason it was lacking was because there was a broad and deep surge of theoretical amalgamation taking place in the councils of scientists of man: that theory and research were being weeded and wedded so as to produce an unmistakable, factual image of man, a clear and agreed portrait of basic human nature. We might imagine all these things because not to imagine them would mean that we are not building any agreed science of man, that whatever progress we might be making in theoretical and empirical work, as solid as it might seem, is being constructed on a base of shifting sand. Without an agreed portrait of basic human nature, our best theoretical and empirical work is rootless, anecdotal, disjointed, peripheral. And even worse: it is based on an image of man that is implicit, disguised, ideological. In a word, it is the erection of a scientific edifice on an unexamined central core, a heap of theory and data that reposes on an unexamined belief.

And yet, such is exactly the state of affairs today. It is distressing. A half-dozen years ago (1962) I wrote a brief essay entitled "Anthropological Notes on the Concept of Aggression," which was an attempt to address this problem of basic human nature. Today I return to it with "Further Notes" that represent some added years of study of the matter. Since the question is so central, it is important to shed as much light as possible on it, even in the absence of dialogue and debate. Perhaps one day it may all be turned to good account. Frankly, I don't very well see how the central problem of a science can continue to be shunted to the periphery of the work of the scientists, no matter how preoccupied they may be. The fact is that the science of man *began* with this question, and must one day return to it—or expire because of betrayed hopes. And the hopes can be betrayed as much by well-intentioned irrelevance, as they can by conscious evasion. Indeed, this is just what we are seeing today, as the central question continues to be avoided. In my previous essay I lamented that the idea of a basically aggressive human nature was an idea that "dies hard." I hinted at that time that the major reason that it dies hard is that the scientists themselves refuse to recognize the corpse. I didn't see how they could carry on their work in a straightforward manner unless they agreed on this matter. Today I know better: straightforwardness in science is an ideal toward which we still aim, and not a condition of daily work.

I have lately written quite a bit on the eighteenth century, as the time when the ideal of a science of man began. The refreshing thing about that time was that the thinkers who sketched the ideal were straightforward in their hopes and aims. They had to be, or else they could not formulate a clear ideal. And they were helped, we know today, by the very fact that there was so little empirical work to cloud their vision: they knew practically nothing so that the argument around basic ideas could be all the more unashamed and unreserved. It was Rousseau, above all, as we know, who argued that man has no basic drives of meanness or aggression; that he is born neutral. And since this was so, a science of man was possible and desirable. Possible, because on the basis of man's neutrality we could educate children to be what we wanted. Desirable, because since children were neutral, and educable, we could finally try to bring about a better world through better education and planning. That was in 1762, when he wrote *Émile*. Today we are no clearer on this problem. What happened in the two hundred years since Rousseau made his claim? Specifically, what do the *empirical* data about children show? Was Rousseau right or wrong? Surely after these many generations of conscientious work, we should have some kind of clear answer. And if we have not, there should surely be some reasonable explanation of our difficulties. Let me try to summarize in a pointed way the highlights of this frustrating dilemma: what the facts show; and why the dilemma is so frustrating, even in the face of more or less clear facts.

The Fate of Rousseau's Intuition

Rousseau's intuition about man's basically neutral nature never achieved an unambiguous ascendancy in the science of man, or any continued ascendancy at all; and for this, there were, I think, four major reasons, which I shall call "Empirical," "Scientific-ideological," "Individual-psychological," and "Scientific-political." Let us examine them in order.

1. *Empirical reasons for the sidetracking of Rousseau's intuition.* Here we invoke the familiar fact of the ascendancy of Darwinism. It took a full century after Rousseau's work to articulate a convincing theory of evolution, a theory which showed that man was unquestionably a member of the animal kingdom. This would not have been news to the eighteenth

century, but it had an unintended effect on their beginning work: after Darwin, all empirical work on man was designed to show his kinship with the antecedent animals; man had to be cogitated as an animal, and his uniqueness had to try to be explained on the same material-causal principles that explained the rest of evolution. This meant that the "clues" to man's nature came to be sought among other animals. And this tradition has continued up to today, with undiminished vigor and resoluteness. So much so, that to talk of "basic human nature" without finding clues for that nature in animal behavior is considered somehow unscientific and unempirical. Not that there is anything wrong with gathering clues where they may be found, but the perverse result is that we are still looking principally to the zoologists for our understanding of man. Witness the wide publicity given to Konrad Lorenz's recent work *On Aggression,* and the excitement and hopes with which scientists of man turn to reading it. Witness the expectations for "real" discovery, attendant upon such ideas as "territoriality" among the lower animals, "social space and distancing" and "display" behavior, or upon primate studies in their natural habitat, and so on. Witness, finally, whole books written around these simple themes, which purport to provide the "key" to man's nature, as in the work of Robert Ardrey—puerile books which should meet the skepticism and scorn they deserve, but which instead find interested and credulous readership even among professionals. We will see some more reasons for this credulousness further on; for now, suffice it to remind ourselves that these works are part of the continuing ascendancy of the great

Darwinian synthesis, and thus have all the legitimation and compellingness of an established scientific tradition and attitude.

It matters little that the best of these empirical studies end with an admission that they may have much to tell us about animals, but for that very fact they have little to tell us about man. We usually overlook the factual conclusions of these studies, as we tacitly accept the premises on which they are based, and continue on about our work. When someone of the roundness and stature of a Lorenz, or a Bertalanffy, tells us that biologists have really little to say about "human" nature, we are inclined to accept this with a gentle disbelief, and consider it a courtesy born of their admirable stature itself. We don't listen to what the men are saying, but rather what they represent.

2. *Scientific-ideological reasons for failing to get clear about man's basic nature.* This second point grows, naturally, from the first. Darwinism unleashed a whole generation of workers who sought to find *the* instincts by which human behavior was governed. If man is an animal, then he must be driven by instincts, *et voilà tout.* We know how instinct theory thrived in the psychology of the early part of this century, and how it gradually died out as a theoretical problem in the 1920's and 1930's. It was only in psychoanalysis that the dogma has been kept alive; and here too, the attacks on and modifications of Freudian libido theory, by psychoanalysts themselves in the past two decades, may mean that it will finally belatedly expire in its last major unexamined stronghold.

Now, as we said, it is logical that an instinctivist view of man should thrive when the dominant scientific ideology is one of

Darwinian naturalism. To see man as a creature who harbors basic drives of sexuality and aggression, like all other animals, is a most direct and acceptable explanation of his behavior. But the instructive fact for us here is a most unusual one. Namely, that the instinctivist view of man did not die out because it confronted the Rousseauian view and was discredited in the factual confrontation. This would have been the scientifically desirable case, but it did not occur, and *has still not occurred.* Instinct theory has been discredited by the best authorities and the most sober-minded empirical work, but this discrediting did not result in the validation of a noninstinctivist approach to human nature. The problem of an image of man, instead of being clarified, was merely evaded. And it was evaded for reasons that are best expressed as scientific-ideological.

In a stimulating historical overview of the instinct doctrine in psychology, Krantz and Allen (1967) point out a very striking fact: namely, that when instinct doctrine lapsed in the late 1920's, it was not ousted by "another theory covering a similar domain of behavior," but rather by a "different approach to social psychology." And this different approach was a narrowing of the scope of social psychology, away from general, synthetic questions to more narrow questions of researchable empirical facts. In other words, social psychology limited its scope and abandoned the search for a general explanation of human motives, which is what the instinct doctrine attempted to provide. We might say that social psychology retrenched its positions to what was most manageable according to the scientific ideology of the time, rather than what was most meaningful for explaining human behavior. I do not have the space here to go into the merits or demerits of this shift of interest in philosophy-of-science terms; suffice it to record the fact that a confrontation and clarification with Rousseau's view was again avoided.

3. *Individual-psychological reasons for a shift in emphasis from larger, more central problems to smaller, more segmented ones.* This third point is itself an outgrowth and a complement to the second: the reasons that scientists follow fads in the first place is partly also a function of their own dispositions, preferences, and limitations. When scientists who should be occupied with broad questions choose narrow ones instead, there is some "psychological gain" involved in the process. This is not an easy matter to be clear about; and it is a very delicate one to generalize about; yet, we can say some general things without fear of unfair distortion.

For one thing, when we phrase our theories of human behavior in narrow terms involving few factors, we phrase them so that many people can understand them. This is one of the main reasons for the popularity of the work of Ardrey, William Golding, and plays such as *The Bad Seed*. To explain human motives on a simple basis like heredity or territoriality gives any *Homo sapiens* with a 1200 cc brain the chance to "understand" his world. We find its equivalent in folk characterology, where someone is "tricky as a fox"—and we know what to expect from him his whole life long. It is what I like to call a "fetishization" of the larger problem, for the sake of facile approach and control. This "fetishization" of large, complex issues, by singling out a narrow, simplistic approach to them, by means of which they may be summed up, is a danger to all of science, to all human explanations. One of the reasons that Freudian theory itself has enjoyed such popularity in both popular and professional minds, is that it provides a relatively "cheap and easy" key to the deep dilemmas of what makes people act the way they do. A few instincts like aggression and sexuality; a universal complex; and then a dark and deep unconscious to explain what cannot otherwise simply be explained: and anyone is the master of human motives. We see this in our psychiatric residency programs, where students trained in medicine can so quickly be made to feel at ease as experts on human behavior: all they have to do is mouth the formulas. The student adopts a simple and schematic view of man, centering around a few basic instincts and mechanisms and a concise new vocabulary loaded with the weight of prestige and legitimated in the world of "hard" clinical practice; and in exchange for this he is offered not only expertise, but more important, peace of mind and relief from the anxiety of his own inadequacy. We see the same things in our graduate schools, when sociology students are offered exemption from the anxious burden of reading Saint-Simon, Fourier, Comte, Marx, and Engels—not to mention Hobbes, Plato, Augustine, and Ibn Khaldun—when they are offered this exemption, as we said, if they will only apply their earlier study of calculus to the mastery of statistical technique. No need to build a library, no need to wrestle with pages and pages of "unintelligible" stuff ("unintelligible" because it contains no charts or graphs, no measurable data). Their instructors tell them: "Just learn the technique of social research, and you can be a Ph.D. and a peer holding a candle to no one, no matter how well-read or rounded he may appear. He is not the 'true scientist';—but you, in virtue of your mastery of statistical techniques, are one of a minority of correct and honest, and admittedly limited but powerful men." So the fatal fetishization is implanted: a locus of scientific control is created, while a larger and more meaningful synthetic scientific picture is hopelessly abandoned.

How does this apply to the problem of man's basic nature? The examples literally stuff our textbooks and research reports, and carry our theory. Everywhere we see how broad and subtle answers are sacrificed to narrow and facile ones. Take the question of aggression itself. In my early paper I tried to show how it was unfairly used as a conceptual scaffolding to hide and distort much larger problems: problems like ego-weakness, the urge to self-esteem, and the opportunities for self-esteem that are made available in any given society. Admittedly, these larger problems are not easy to research or to convey to others. But when we falsify them by fetishizing our research problem, we distort the empirical reality, no matter how "careful and scientific" this distortion may be. When we talk, for example, about basic instincts that are responsible for the hate and war that plague this planet, just how much do we explain a *particular* war? If we talk about "territorial imperatives" and the inviolability of the urge to private property, how well do these concepts serve to scaffold our explanations over why we are in Vietnam? The popular imagination takes refuge in an image of man that shows him to be mean and vicious because such an image easily explains all the world ills at one swoop. If you say that man is a wolf or a fox, then everyone becomes a philosopher about the human condition and can nod his head wisely behind bolted doors. But broad and deep-going explanations of the causes of World War I and II require a broad knowledge of history and social theory. Even more, they require a complete honesty about the political motivations of one's own country. Few people can marshal these things, can talk in terms of military-industrial complexes, of big-statism, the power ideology of nationalism, the identification of the masses with the power of the leader, and so on. Fewer still would want to, which is why we have been able to identify "fetishization" in science as a function of "bourgeois science" in general: it destroys the total picture by narrowing it down, because the total picture would itself contain a blistering critique of some of the basic institutions that sustain the hordes of busy scientists. And today we know that "bourgeois science" not only characterizes most of the work in Western countries, but in Communist ones as well.

Of course, the problem of fetishization in science is part of the problem of fetishization in life as a whole: we all fetishize to a certain extent—indeed we must, else we could not carry on. Our control over the multiform drama of personal, social, political, local and world events is so limited; at the same time, our ability to keep these multiform processes in our minds and emotions, and so let them trouble us, is virtually limitless. We can even get personally upset about "contaminating" the moon with earthly bacteria. Obviously, this lopsided situation of almost complete projection of the self into the world and into other worlds, while at the same time having our controls limited to one finite animal organism, needs some kind of redress. And this redress, as we said, is "creative fetishization": the singling out only of those preoccupations which are in the purview of our control. As Schopenhauer so well put it: I shall only be concerned about those things that are in my power to alter. It is a kind of deliberate self-retrenchment or self-abasement, and in a sense, a paradoxical creation of a "fantasy" realm of "real" control—we might call it a voluntary type of mental illness. It led one of my psychiatrist friends to remark in all seriousness: "A little mental illness [fetishization] goes a long way [to keep mental health]." The thing is very plain. We all do it—the more consciously and deliberately and self-critically, the better.

But it takes its toll of scientific understanding, which is why we call the problem we are discussing the "individual-psychological" dimension of distortion of the theory of basic human nature. Most often this is, of course, done unwittingly and innocently: people see what they are capable of seeing, what they want to see. It is a function of automatic and benign habitual repression. But look what it does to theory. We take a simple word like "aggression" and we use it to scaffold a whole field of understanding, simply because it is easy for us to do so and because it gives us such comforting command over a world of disparate and puzzling occurrences. When a child breaks a vase, the Freudian sees "aggression." When he fondles his genitals at an age when he has no real consciousness that the lower part of his body belongs to him or has any functions that pertain to him, the Freudian sees "sexuality" and "incest wishes." When someone with a weak and insecure ego blushes constantly in public, the Freudian sees a sign that the person is trying to cover up deep surges of aggression and urges to kill—hence he blushes at this revelation of his own murderousness, etc. The Freudians saw sex and aggression everywhere they looked, and are only lately beginning to come out of it. One wonders what the Victorian Freud had on his mind when he looked at infants: how he could possibly read sexual motivations into their innocent self-fondling and aimless curiosity. I know several nice old ladies who would call Freud "a very nasty man"—and they would be right. Today we know that Freud read into his cases motivations that probably were not there. We know too that children manifest aggressive behavior with the most innocent of motives—like trying to get attention, or trying to keep action moving forward, without any sure formulas for such action. Rousseau saw that a child will break a vase because he is clumsy, *tout court,* and doesn't know how to relate to a vase. One has only to watch children without preconceptions to accept this view of their basic innocence and neutrality; one has only to see in their impulses and struggles the ineptitude that is born of weakness and limitation. This is just the kind of view that is spreading in studies today (cf. Burks and Harrison, 1962), and the facile fetishization of words like "aggression" is being discarded as empirically inadequate and distorting.

The Freudians can and probably will continue to oversimplify the world of human motivations for their patients, but at least scientists of man in the broad sense need not get bogged down in the confined traffic of consultation rooms. What serious student of human nature has not been moved to rage when some overwhelmed and perplexed person undergoing Freudian analysis had to give tearful vent to the suffocating air they were breathing in the closed world of Freudian fantasy? They were given a Freudian vocabulary to apply to their desires and fears, and they literally fetishized their world by thinking in terms of penis envy, the desire to kill the father, castration fears, and whatnot. Of course, the vocabulary "works"—and this is the tragedy. If we accept to think in Freudian terms, we can analyze our lives in those terms—we can *shape ourselves* into those terms. And it "works"—but it also risks driving us crazy, as any extreme and unreal fetishization will. Use a paranoid vocabulary and you become paranoid, as our political leaders are teaching us today. Use a sexual vocabulary and you can live and feel and act out your life on sexual terms, as most of us have done at certain times. The deeper question is, what is the nature of reality and what are our real desires? And this question is harder to answer.

The Freudian who talks inanely about pathological blushing as a reaction to the fear of killing (Feldman, 1962) would have to substitute a phenomenological theory of blushing, such as the great Max Scheler adumbrated. But this kind of under-standing requires breadth, learning, and time—and these are not available in the crowded medical curriculum, or in the busy and practical psychiatric residency. To see the world of the child as Rousseau and his followers saw it, and as sensitive

researchers are again beginning to see it today, requires a
freedom from preconceptions, an innocent passivity on one's
own part, a broad learning in the relativity of cultural behavior.
It requires, in a word, a general theory of human behavior, not
a Freudian one. And this kind of theory is not the one taught
in Freudian schools of analysis. (We will touch below on the
truly great things that Freudian thought discovered, but these
things are not the ones given basic attention in the everyday
dogma.) Also indispensable to this general theory is some
familiarity with ontology: we could then understand why children will push and pull to affirm their organisms, why they
will rival with their siblings for attention, why men in general
will try to maximize their own importance and their power.
And the reason is not that people are born with drives of hate
or aggression, but rather that man as an *energy-converting and
purposive organism* seeks the maximization of his own being,
of his own sense of self.[1] When neutral organisms seek to expand their self-feeling and to extend their control, they must
needs do so in some way in competition with or at the obvious
expense of their fellows. And this makes them seem "motivated"
by antisocial desires. But the ontological ground is neutral, not
in itself destructive. This is the important point. Recently Mumford has pointedly summed up the whole of human history:
Man is not a tool-user primarily who seeks to manipulate the
world, but a self-maximizer who seeks to expand his experience
in composite ways. But in order to cogitate about man in these
terms, one would need not only Mumford's broadness but one
would need to substitute a critique of man's social forms for a

discursus on human nature. I mean that if man is a neutral self-maximizer and not a hateful destroyer of his fellow man, it is up to councils of men to modify social customs so as to allow creative expansion of being. And it is in the face of this kind of hurdle that we draw the circle on our discussion: scientific fetishization, as we said, is a reflex of bourgeois science. It is easier to find the evil in man's animal nature than in one's social world—easier both personally and socially. This leads us to our final point.

4. *The scientific-political reason for the failure to confront Rousseau's view of man.* In a sense this is the most complex point of all, and we can do no better than to take ourselves back in time to when Rousseau's view *was* first confronted by his contemporary, the brilliant Helvétius. In his important work *On Man* (1772), Helvétius says the following things in opposition to Rousseau, things which clarify immediately this whole long and complex problem, and allow us to state it in terms most meaningful to present-day debate.

> "Woe to the prince who trusts in the basic goodness of people. Mr. Rousseau believes it, but experience belies it. Whoever consults experience learns that the child drowns flies, beats his dog, suffocates his sparrow, and that, born without innate ideas, the child has all the vices of the adult. By force he appropriates his friend's goodies and jewels; in order to gain a doll he does what in ripe age one does for a title or a throne" (1772, p. 219, my translation).

One curious fact about this denial of Rousseau's views is that Rousseau did not maintain that man is basically good, but rather neutral—a position that Helvétius himself earlier maintains. He sees that man is born a *tabula rasa* as in Locke's view, and that children become by interacting with human objects (p. 217). The burden of Helvétius's discomfort with Rousseau is elsewhere, and it is soon obvious what the real gravamen of his dispute is: he is not so much concerned with the way man *is,* but rather with something more *political,* namely, with the kind of conduct *that would result* if one stressed man's elemental goodness or badness. If we *say* men *are* good, says Helvétius, they will be induced to act bad. Therefore we must be careful about our scientific pronouncements: they translate into political and social acts. This is what really troubled Helvétius, and what is really at the heart of our disagreements in large areas of social theory today.

What Helvétius reveals is that the problem of basic human nature cannot be decided purely on scientific grounds. It is a pragmatic problem as well, since it depends on the kind of world we want to live in and want to or can bring about. The choice of whether man is basically good or bad is itself *a self-fulfilling prophecy:* man can be aggressive when he seeks to maximize his sense of being at the expense of flies, dogs, and sparrows, or at that of weaker playmates in competition for toys. As an adult he can ply these behaviors in more serious matters, at the expense of large groups of his fellow man. On the other hand, if suitable social channels and arrangements are made available, then self-maximization can be accomplished in sport, in competitions in the arts, crafts, and social service. William James knew these things when he called for a peaceful "moral equivalent" of war: men had energy to burn in their urge to self-enhancement. It was up to society to provide life-ways that make this self-enhancement creative rather than socially destructive.

When society does not make such provision, then we can actually say that it is responsible for man's aggressive and destructive outbursts. Where world law and world government do not exist, Olympic games are eclipsed by world wars. Our experience on these matters has been so pointed and bitter, that even my talking in such vague generalities must carry enough conviction to men of good will. Even a "conservative" social theorist like Parsons could pen a trenchant essay on this problem (1947). Choose that man must be curbed by law, because of his innate destructiveness, bottle him up in ghettos and deny him the opportunity to enhance his sense of self—and he will be curbed by law because of innate destructiveness. Choose that man is potentially good if we adapt our institutions to the expression of free creativity, and we will bring about a better type of person. We have only to recall the rehabilitation programs for children who have been brought up as "bad" in order to see how they can become "good" when the channels for socially-benevolent behavior are provided, and when their own image is changed. In sum, our theory on the nature of man is in large part a self-fulfilling prophecy. Take your pick —utopian or anti-utopian, and your world will be molded accordingly. Rousseau knew this as well as Helvétius, only he had a more trusting view of human nature as well as a more subtle understanding of what was in back of ostensible childhood destructions.[2]

And yet there is something still deeper behind this difference between the two men, and it is important to dwell on it. As we said, it runs through social theory today. We see it in the juxtaposition of men like Daniel Bell, Edward Shils, Talcott Parsons, and Neil Smelser on one hand, and C. Wright Mills, John R. Seeley, and Edgar Friedenberg, on the other. We see it in the reviews they write of each other's books, we see it in the type of their social thought, and it is unmistakable. It is an opposition which can best be summed up as a case of Hobbes versus Rousseau, as the politics of a particular world view and personal option. On the Hobbesian hand, we have people who stand for *perpetuation.* These are the institutionalists, the men who seek the rule of law, the perpetuation of order, the continuity and durability of the *proven forms* of social arrangements. They believe that the forms of things have to be maintained, even over and against the wishes of segments of people. People, to their mind, are in some ways dangerous, and must be protected against themselves. People need orderly institutions, whether they acknowledge it or not, and when they run afoul of these institutions, it is the people who must bend. Innovation is dangerous, and hard to control; it has unforeseeable effects, and cannot be left to the whims of men. Institutional process is the thing, the best guide for social life: it levels and absorbs, and blunts potential destruction. Utopias are unreal as well as dangerous, impractical as well as upsetting. So deep is this option on the part of some of these men that, like Smelser, they would trust in the institutions and work against abrupt changes, even in a post-atomic-holocaust world.

It seems that even total failure is acceptable, so long as it is organized by the majority of men, against the unreal and untried visions of the few.

On the other or Rousseauian hand, we have the *charismatics,* who are opposed to the institutional perpetuators. These men believe that hope lies in the new, in innovations. They believe that the center of truthfulness lies in individual subjectivities rather than in the objective network of institutions. They see quality in the new and untried, more than in the habitual. They trust individuals, favor the experimentation by minorities, are willing to risk unorganized success. They believe that the few may be able to save the many, even from themselves. In sameness and continuity they see and feel the forebodings of real disaster; in innovation they sense rebirth and the promise of victory. Where their opponents might invoke the Koran and the Talmud, the rule of law over the passions of men, they might invoke Christ and the new birth, the innocence and saving grace of the untried.

The juxtaposition of these two viewpoints may be trite, but it represents a dichotomy which is very real and deep-going. And it invites judgment: Who is right? Obviously the answer can exclude neither side. The perpetuators are right: society needs institutions, and the main task of man is to stand fast, to carry on. Nature herself perpetuates; it is the only sure thing that we know. For some reason life must hang on; the generations endure. But the perpetuators are wrong to imagine that institutions cannot be their own undoing; they forget that outmoded lifeways can be more dangerous than wishful innovation.

History is strewn with examples of the failure of whole civilizations because of incrusted habitual ways. If nature endures, she endures in order to change. Innovation is a fact of the natural world; the generations last in order to give birth to new generations, to unknown energies. The institutionalists want only to "last out"; the charismatics want to "foresee in order to forestall." The hope of the science of man, especially in the work of its great forebears Saint-Simon, Comte, Durkheim, was that some compromise could be made between the two sides, that they could be harmoniously blended. In other words, if the science of man itself has any meaning, it exists in order to have some influence on institutional change.

Here is the crux of the matter: the science of man is an active, innovative, interventionist science. It is founded on the belief that man must continually modify cherished lifeways to accord with future goals and continuing historical changes. If this science is to be a central fact of modern life, then the balance must swing to the innovators. If this science is to be peripheral and impotent, then, of course, all we can do is to "endure" and preserve our institutions as best we can. Ultimately, only a philosophy of history can tell us who is right, since it would tell us the meaning of the whole historical process. But scientists themselves, who live off a tradition and way of life, cannot wait for such a philosophy to guide their efforts. Neither can their aim be to stand fast. The great contradiction at the heart of the institutionalist position is that they want their scientific cake and the sameness of their institutions too. And it is this timidity and self-negating compromise which makes them seem increasingly pathetic, amoral, and villainous to the young social scientists.

And so we can conclude this part of our discussion, the *scientific-political* obstructions to an agreed image of man. We can see that agreement over such an image implies a plan of action, a type of investment in the external world: either a commitment to act innovatively, or not to act. Rousseau has been shunted aside here, simply because the Hobbesians have been firmly entrenched in power in the social sciences since the very beginning of the formation of their disciplines in the latter part of the nineteenth century, and the early part of the twentieth. Thus, for them, it has not been a question of who is right, but of who has the power to impose a particular image on a science. Undoubtedly part of their fear of the charismatics is hardly personally disinterested: the charismatics threaten not only general social order for the masses, but the accustomed disposal of power and privilege in the realm of science itself. To be against charisma in science is at the same time to be for the continued institutionalization of one's own control over the conduct, finances, and perquisites of the whole of social science. Imagine filling department chairmanships with students of C. Wright Mills, rather than of Lazarsfeld! It sends a shudder through the whole edifice of contemporary social science.

Conclusion

So much for our brief review of some of the main ideological and psychological reasons for failing to place an agreed image of man at the center of social science. To many students these questions are annoying in their relativity, in their frank rooting in the context of power, opportunity, and fiat. Surely science is more than this, surely there is a main thrust of theory that draws its legitimation from empirical fact, they will argue, and correctly. We began our discussion by showing the major empirical reason for the sidestepping of Rousseau's intuition, namely, the solidity and ascendancy of Darwinian naturalism. Any argument that seeks to place an agreed image of man in the center of science must deal with this naturalistic, empirical tradition. But having come this far, we can see that the question has to be rephrased: *not,* what are the empirical objections to Rousseau (since we see that there are none that carry irrefragable weight), but rather, the question now becomes: what are the empirical data that might support Rousseau's intuition, if we place aside the relative problems of individual psychology and ideology in science?

Given the tradition of scientific naturalism to which we must cling, there are some basic conditions which our empirical support of Rousseau must fulfill. The primary one is that basic human nature must be explained on the grounds of man's place in the animal kingdom; but this explanation cannot reduce man to specific and simple animal drives. The reason, we have seen, is that man does not have absolute drives that work against the hope of peaceful, harmonious society. Even those drives that man has in a higher degree than the other animals—such as year-round sexual hormonal tonus—are highly modifiable. As for drives like hunger, sleep, comfort, and so on, which are normally considered irreducible instincts, we omit them from our purview here for the simple reason that they do not make for disharmony in social life except under unusual crisis conditions. We have not been able to discover that man has specific antisocial drives that are modifiable only with difficulty and with a residue of bitterness and personal deprivation, as Freud thought. Yet, we must keep our accent on man as an energy-converting organism who follows general laws of organismic behavior, and who comes to direct this behavior—albeit clumsily—by means of symbols.

Another way of putting this is that we must show how man's inhumanity to man can take place on the basis of a fundamental *organismic neutrality* of basic striving—we must explain human evil nonspecifically just as we explain the predatory behavior of animals specifically. While this task seems formidable to the biologists and those who take their cues from them, it is really very simple and straightforward to the social scientist who bases his theory on what is durable in the traditions of Marx and Freud.

I have spent considerable space on this problem in other writings, and there is hardly any point in repeating in these notes what I have covered at length elsewhere. Also, let us remember some of the points we made above on the ineptitude of the child's behavior and especially on the ontological dimension of human striving: all organisms seek the maximization of being in relation to the full field of objects. Dante had some beautiful lines to say about this, as did Goethe: the striving organism revels in the consciousness of its free power and in its overcoming of obstacles. But it is only when we turn to what is durable in Freud that we can understand how this translates into the peculiar problem of human evil. In all my quarrels with the remnants of instinct theory in Freud, I am perhaps guilty of carping about his genius, of not giving his stature its due. Partly this has been unavoidable, since there is much in Freud that is sheer nonsense. Partly it is ludicrous to try to shackle a man of his greatness to points of specific fallibility, when his contribution has been so world-historically important. If I have been guilty of such ludicrousness let me apologize for it now by trying to show what exactly seems durable in Freud.

Two major things, I think. The first is the idea of the Oedipus complex; not perhaps in the sense in which he intended it, but rather as it has been distilled from the whole corpus of psychoanalytic literature in all the various schools. The Oedipus complex really shows one fundamental thing, and it is a general thing, not the specific thing that Freud wanted to show. Oedipus means simply that all members of *Homo sapiens* undergo a childhood training in which is implanted an automatic style of behavior guided by symbols—an uncritical world view inculcated by the parent trainers of the young.

The second, and related thing, is that since this world view is uncritical, it is unreflective: we do not *know* why we have the sense of right and wrong that we have—we act on it, feel it, live it, and believe it. We are the prisoners of our early-implanted sense of conscience. And this is what we mean by the Unconscious. The Unconscious is not a reservoir of animal drives; rather, it is the unexamined residue of our early training and feeling about ourselves and the world. Since the Unconscious represents our basic organismic conditioning about the kind of world we are comfortable in, the kind that is "right and true" for us; we must understand that it comprises the gross and deep-going *motives* of our behavior—motives which are not amenable to reflective, symbolic scrutiny. Since our Unconscious is our basic emotional identification with the kinds of feelings and acts which make us comfortable, we can say that it contains the motives that *determine* our behavior, whether we consciously will it or not. It was thus easy for Freud to be overly specific about the Unconscious: to see it as a reservoir of hopelessly antisocial motives, motives that predate the human condition itself. But this link into the recesses of evolution is an unnecessary and false theoretical closure. Whatever else the Unconscious may be, biologically or even ontologically, the social scientist must understand it as the *social* artifact which it largely is. Whatever may be happening in the physiochemistry of the cells, or whatever may be linking the cells with another dimension from which they sprang, these facts do not change the primary area of human concern: the formation of the Unconscious in the early *human* training of the organism.

One related and crucial aspect of this early training is that by means of it, the individual earns his sense of self and his right to live and act in society. In other words, each individual earns his right to exist as a social-cultural animal from others of his kind—others who are for many years in a position of superior power to himself, and who usher him into a superordinate symbolic action world. The effects of this cannot be underestimated, as the great Alfred Adler especially taught us. It means that the Unconscious represents our basic rooting in *a source of power* which gives our very life its mandate. This power comes from outside us; it sustains us, justifies us, dwarfs us in some or many ways. Finally, its superordinacy over us is not amenable to symbolic scrutiny: even worse, the words that we learn from others are largely a disguise and a justification of our basic power allegiance. And so we can well understand why Freud gave the Unconscious such a prominent place in his theory, and why he thought of most people as "trash": they are simple reflexes of their early anxieties, who learn to ply their secondhand motives with a pathetic righteousness—as though they were standing on their own, and knew the way things are.

We must emphasize, too, how deep-going this process is: it helps us to understand the difficulty of real growth and the anguish of conversion to a new world view. The fundamental fact about each human being is that his early growth is in large part a denial and masking of his anxiety, his powerlessness, his felt finitude. If we shouted this knowledge from the rooftops and over loud-speakers, we could still not stress it enough. How well the great Kierkegaard understood this long ago. And how well, too, he understood that one cannot really grow in later life unless one throws off this mask, this denial, and comes face to face with his utter helplessness and impotence toward natural forces. But to admit this is not merely a verbal matter: it means throwing aside everything that the wide-eyed child has painfully and gradually built up over the years: the armor of self-assurance borrowed from people and powers around him that makes his life livable in a somewhat carefree way. This is why organisms can't really change fundamentally unless they break down emotionally, and experience the bankruptcy of their borrowed powers. *The whole cast of one's muscles and nerves is shaped as a denial of his real insignificance.* And this organismic denial is what must be broken down in order for real growth to take place. In this basic sense, then, we must insist that the whole social formation of man's physical organism, and the veneer of symbols which cloaks its striving, is a *vital lie.* In order for the person to get back to his place on the cutting edge of evolution he must expose this lie by admitting the primal physical fear and trembling that it covers. False courage would then vanish, and the individual would begin to see things as they really are in relation to himself, and not as he has imagined them for his automatic comfort. He might be disillusioned, ejected from his stage-prop paradise, but at least he would be "his own" person and no longer a puppet jerked about by alien powers.

Elsewhere I wrote that motives are words, that words guide and shape our conduct. I wrote this to promote the symbolic-interactionist view of man, which stressed the hope that reason and light can be the guiding forces over human conduct. Freud meant the same thing when he said that the voice of the Ego, while soft, continues until it is heard. But the fact is, as Freud knew, that most of the time and for most people, this voice is not heard. This means that motives remain unknown and disguised by words. It means that only *ideally* are motives words:

ideally one would hope to place his primary reliance on the free flow of symbols that would guide his choices, and allow him to weigh them before acting. But this is ideal. Actually, man acts, and then masks his action in the automatic justification of words. He manufactures a seemly vocabulary to justify what he *must* do. The organismic cast and thrust has been molded by anxieties and identifications which continually interfere with the free flow of thought and perception. This explains the perplexing fact of why most people talk past each other when they seek to convince one another. Words will not shake their basic power allegiances, when these allegiances are to different sources of power, to different feelings about how the world ought to be, about who is really right and in control, about the kind of people who will win and ought to win.

And so we have complex human organisms that strive to maximize their being, and who do so by uncritical allegiances to different sources of sustaining power. Small wonder that the world is in a whirl, that man is a "wolf unto man." It was Konrad Lorenz who somewhere pointed out how fallacious this analogy with the wolves is: among wolves there is an automatic instinctual mechanism that prevents them from killing each other off. The wolf who is losing a fight merely tends his jugular vein to the stronger one, and this automatically renders the stronger one impotent to press to the kill. No such instincts among man, hence the bloodshed—a bloodshed by self-maximizing organisms who are rooted emotionally in very personal mandates for their existence. Since no two people are rooted in exactly the same murky complex of self-sustenance, each is on his own, and blood relationship itself is as airy as a symbol to prevent mutual slaughter. Brother feeds on brother.

Of course, man's "primate nature" has something to do with this subservience to a stronger outside source of power: it looks much akin to the dominance-hierarchies of baboons and the great apes. But this does not explain it: we see it too among dogs and other mammals. It seems to be a characteristic of all organisms who are immersed in a transcendent nature, and must draw their limited powers in a feeble dependence on an encompassing world. In other words, it is general, neutral, and nonspecific. To say too, that like other primates man has a sense of territory and will fight to the death to protect his brood, is again to say very little about the general range of his aggressive behavior. How many specific individuals do we know in the course of our own lives who have died defending their home plot of land? Even in history it is a rare enough event to move us—as at Thermopylae and in aboriginal North America. To say that we are deeply moved over this because we share the nature of primates is at best anecdotal: it covers a small segment of the rivers of human blood that man has shed. Do we have to state the obvious, and say that we have long known what causes armies of men to march to slaughter and genocide? It is not man's aggressiveness, but rather his fearfulness and automatic submissiveness to authority. This is the sickness at the heart of the creature, that makes him so terrible in the animal kingdom: he spills blood out of weakness.

Human evil, we may finally conclude, is self-created, not animal-inspired. It springs from the ground of restless striving that characterizes all organisms. The uniqueness of man is that, with reason and thought, he might have a different destiny if he could but see through his Oedipus or early training, and come to identify the unconscious rooting of his own sense of self. This is what Freud taught us, and this is precisely where he and Rousseau meet: "Basic Human Nature" is a blank slate, an ideal of self-fashioning and self-development, an ideal offered peculiarly and uniquely to man. An ideal of individual life, as Freud saw; and an ideal of social theory, as Rousseau wanted. Whether man has the wisdom and the luck on this earthly career to be able to reach for such an ideal, is something which will probably be decided in the next few decades. At least, for us—scientists of man—let it be recorded that we knew our subject matter; that we understood the limitations of our powers to fashion an agreed science. Then, if we do meet eventual defeat, it will be in the same manner as the best of the ancient Greeks: in the dignity of having achieved the best that we could in the face of our ineluctable fate.

AUGUST, 1967

Notes

1. It is very important to note here something that properly belongs under point two, above: that, historically, human behavior began to be explained in terms of instincts partly because psychology wanted the prestige of an independent scientific discipline. The idea of instincts allowed us to explain behavior on a basis of individual psychology, and thus tore psychology away from both philosophy and sociology. But then the great paradox occurred: instinct theory itself was discredited and abandoned, and there was now no way to explain individual purposive behavior: without instincts, we could no longer theorize, within the confines of the single discipline of materialist psychology, about basic human motivations! And so the circle was complete: having abandoned ontology and sociology, academic disciplinary psychology had next to abandon hope of explaining human behavior. Its justification as a discipline could only be maintained by the mask of careful empirical research on more segmented problems, which mask it indeed did don. See Krantz and Allen, 1967; and cf. also E. Becker, *The Structure of Evil*, Braziller: 1968.

2. It is instructive to compare how closely this basic scientific question in the science of man parallels the same process in the "harder" sciences. For example, we ask: "If we meet man's need for self-maximizing activity and a basic feeling of worth, will he still be destructively aggressive?" The physicist asks: "If we change the field in which particle Y moves, how will particle Y act? Is it fated to act in that way—what is the unflinchable law, and how can it be applied?" The only problem for the scientist of man is that his society *does not want to intervene* in the total field. Thus, he can hardly begin to get the kind of laws that the physicist gets, who constantly manipulates the total field of his objects. This is the reason,

too, that the scientist of man has been the last to appreciate the lessons of philosophy since Kant: he continues to want to know things "as they really are," in themselves, simply because he forfeits the right to know them in their variable relationships to a whole field of forces. In terms of our previous discussion, we might say that since he cannot get a broad picture of relative, interdependent truths, he fetishizes his search to a narrow picture of Absolute, Independent Truth. The result is a Babel of superstitions and ideologies about human nature, and an utter failure to proceed to a science of man in society: people want to know *exactly* what man is before any move can be made into the venturesomeness of scientific planning.

Also, let us note another fetishization in the science of human affairs that is not found in the "hard" sciences it so much claims to admire. Supposing that we were to provide for new conditions of life that would diminish aggressiveness in society by an overwhelming percentage. Would isolated cases of aggressiveness count as proof against our Rousseauian theory of human nature? The conservatives say it would. But scientifically the single case exception has no validity in disproving the basic theory. The conservative bases his judgment on striking cases of human evil; but scientifically, the striking case has no weight, when the statistical average favors the general theoretical postulates. This is another instance of the search for Absolute and Unexceptionable Truth, a search that fouls the whole venture of science. The conservative cannot imagine a Utopia without sex criminals and psychopaths, and so abandons the idea of working for a better society. This is the fanaticism of Absolutism.

References

Becker, E. (1962), "Anthropological Notes on the Concept of Aggression" *Psychiatry: Journal for the Study of Interpersonal Behavioral Sciences,* Vol. 3, pp. 326–38.

Burks, H. L. and Harrison, S. I. (1962), "Aggressive Behavior as a Means of Avoiding Depression" *American Journal of Orthopsychiatry,* Vol. 32, April, pp. 416–22.

Feldman, S. S. (1962), "Blushing, Fear of Blushing, and Shame" *Journal of the American Psychoanalytic Association,* Vol. 10, pp. 368–85.

Helvétius, C. A. (1772), *De l'homme* (Paris: Mercure de France edition, 1909).

Krantz, D. L. and Allen, D. (1967), "The Rise and Fall of McDougall's Instinct Doctrine" *Journal of the History of the Behavioral Sciences,* Vol. 3, pp. 326–38.

Parsons, T. (1947), "Certain Primary Sources and Patterns of Aggression in the Social Structure of the Western World" in *Essays in Sociological Theory,* revised edition (New York: Free Press, 1954), pp. 298–322.

Index